COMFORTS

of the

ABYSS

COMFORTS

of the

ABYSS

THE ART OF PERSONA WRITING

PHILIP SCHULTZ

W. W. NORTON & COMPANY

Independent Publishers Since 1923

For information about permission to reproduce selections from this book,
write to Permissions, W. W. Norton & Company, Inc.,
500 Fifth Avenue, New York, NY 10110

For information about special discounts for bulk purchases, please contact
W. W. Norton Special Sales at specialsales@wwnorton.com or 800-233-4830

Manufacturing by Lakeside Book Company
Book design by Beth Steidle
Production manager: Beth Steidle

Library of Congress Cataloging-in-Publication Data

Names: Schultz, Philip, author.
Title: Comforts of the abyss : the art of persona writing / Philip Schultz.
Description: First edition. | New York, NY : W. W. Norton & Company, [2022]
Identifiers: LCCN 2021061122 | ISBN 9780393531848 (hardcover) | ISBN
9780393531855 (epub)
Subjects: LCSH: Schultz, Philip. | Authorship—Philosophy. | Poets, American—
20th century—Biography. | Poets, American—21st century—Biography. |
Creation (Literary, artistic, etc.)
Classification: LCC PS3569.C5533 Z46 2022 | DDC 811/.54 [B]—dc23/eng/20220214
LC record available at https://lccn.loc.gov/2021061122

W. W. Norton & Company, Inc., 500 Fifth Avenue, New York, N.Y. 10110
www.wwnorton.com

W. W. Norton & Company Ltd., 15 Carlisle Street, London W1D 3BS

1 2 3 4 5 6 7 8 9 0

*For Monica, who, believing the world a better place
when people are creative, helped create this idea
and school*

*And for all our students and teachers who turned a
vision into a reality*

*It is true that negation is the mind's first freedom, yet
a negative habit is fruitful only so long as we exert
ourselves to overcome it, adapt it to our needs; once
acquired it can imprison us—a chain like any other.
And slavery for slavery, the servitude of existence is
the preferable choice, even at the price of a certain self-
splintering: it is a matter of avoiding the contagion of
nothingness, the comforts of the abyss.*

—E. M. CIORAN

*Emotion, which is suffering, ceases to be suffering as
soon as we form a clear and precise picture of it.*

—SPINOZA

*Success, like happiness, cannot be pursued; it must
ensue, and it only does so as the unintended side-effect
of one's dedication to a cause greater than oneself or
as the by-product of one's surrender to a person other
than oneself.*

—VIKTOR E. FRANKL

*All happiness in life depends on having the energy to
assume the mask of some other self.*

—W. B. YEATS

CONTENTS

THE MIND'S FIRST FREEDOM

The Writers Studio was imagined and cobbled together, idea by idea, and mistake by mistake, over the past thirty-five years. I could easily enough claim that its main concept—that of persona writing, or borrowing another writer's narrator, his or her personality, attitude, and tone, and filtering one's own emotions and story through, say, the lusty bravado of a Walt Whitman or Ernest Hemingway, the ironic whimsy of an Isaac Babel, or the intensely focused and radical agitation of an Emily Dickinson or Elizabeth Bishop—evolved out of my early love of first-person narrators. This extra layer of sympathy and confidence affected me as a reader as well as a writer. The writer began to look at whatever I was attempting to say in a more objective and discerning way, and the reader would often forget that I was reading altogether and take on the very persona that was telling me one of these extraordinary stories and poems to the extent that I'd go around pretending I was Jake Barnes in *The Sun Also Rises* and Holden Caulfield in *The Catcher in the Rye*, and even old Huck Finn in *Adventures of Huckleberry Finn*. Their opinions and attitudes became mine, and I would even try to talk and act the way I imagined they did. Which wasn't an easy feat for a dyslexic. I didn't know that I was dyslexic until much later, or that it was the reason I didn't learn to read until I was eleven, was held back twice, and grew up thinking

I was dumb, but this way of reading and seeing the often-confusing world around me allowed me to see myself as a character in stories I wanted to not only read but write.

The writing process is seldom logical, and writers of any seriousness often enough see themselves as unabridged and curious creatures, desirous of the very thing they fear most: exposure of any kind. I know now that if I'm not made uncomfortable by something I'm writing I'm probably not saying anything of value, that true emotional connection almost always creates anxiety. Why else would I need to investigate every thought and act, remain stubbornly suspicious of every desire and surprise, of even my very motivation to create? Isn't it only reasonable that I should feel like a stranger to myself, knowing that the excitement I seek in revelation is matched with dread of equal, if not superior, strength? That this is what the great project of creative thinking is all about, finally, knowing and revealing our incapacities and most intimate thoughts in a cautionary tale we tell ourselves when we think no one else is listening? Isn't this what all the masters were about, too—Henry James, Tolstoy, George Eliot, Shakespeare, Gerard Manley Hopkins, and most certainly Walt Whitman—performing on their psyches surgeries of such magical persuasion they were willing to bring forth what they may have perceived as shameful and pathetic, to disrupt their most intimate sense of privacy and contentment?

And what is it exactly that's being exposed?

"It is true that negation is the mind's first freedom," E. M. Cioran, the brilliant Carpathian philosopher, tells us in his wonderfully dark and powerful study of alienation and futility, *The Temptation to Exist*, "negation being a negative habit . . . fruitful only so long as we exert ourselves to overcome it, adapt it to our needs." I was moved by these words long before I understood them, or my perverse fascination with my own negativity and feelings of fragility and hopelessness. A friend, Ralph Dickey, who attempted to introduce me to a more esoteric world of literature long before I understood why I was so resistant to reading any more than what seemed essential or necessary, first told me about Cioran in a letter he wrote in 1970:

"Maybe I'll xerox it [*Temptation to Exist*] and send it to you. . . . You should buy or steal copies of his [E. M. Cioran's] books. . . . He is brilliant, if nothing else, well horrifying too. And he's probably right in his fundamental argument—that consciousness is a disease—because he's right at almost every point along the way." He was constantly giving me books to read ("I want to send you the whole world, Phillip, and say, 'What do you think?' "). We were each in our own way attempting to illuminate the world of darkness that lived in us with literature and our writing and it's more than ironic that I should find the title for this book in a book he first told me about nearly fifty years ago. Ironic and beautifully fitting.

As a child I often felt as if I were living someone else's life, a kind of apprenticeship to someone I was supposed to be or become, that I was in fact only borrowing my personality, living in servitude to a force or authority greater than myself. This sense of displacement only grew stronger when, at eighteen, I witnessed my father's slow, resolute self-destruction one small, consistent disappointment and business failure at a time. And years after Ralph slowly and painfully succumbed to what he saw as the irresistible allure of his self-loathing, I too became aware of my own infatuation with what Cioran called "the servitude of existence . . . the comforts of the abyss," and began to wonder what would happen if, instead of denying the embrace of this negative force, our very hunger for servitude, one used it as a source of inspiration and creativity. Failure, which played so large a role in my father's life and in my own undiagnosed dyslexic flounderings, eventually became a source of creative strategy and intuition, a subject to draw and paint, and later to write poems and stories about; a means of turning my "self-splintering" into a method of survival and comfort.

Every writer and artist—every human being—is familiar with this dark presence, whose sole purpose is the diminishment of the self, to undermine and discourage our every attempt to distinguish ourselves, to instill fear, doubt, and anger in our every thought, to censor and curtail our every creative desire so we'll continue to play it safe, and sit there, in the dark, remembering all the things we didn't have the presence of mind or courage to say or do in our defense, all the things we can't bring ourselves to forget or forgive—the voice that endlessly second-guesses our good intentions, casts doubts on all the reasons why we should even desire to exist. It's no longer hard to recognize it after every sign of recognition or success, whispering its dark little secrets in my ear, the biggest being its identity, which is perhaps why it camouflages its voice, wanting us to think this pinched, tinny voice is our own, that it's only us thinking all these dark, negative thoughts about something we wrote or said, wanting us to believe that we're only being realistic about our abilities, that this caustic, unsympathetic voice is just trying to protect us from further harm, further shame.

Yes, Cioran got it perfectly right, knowing that the only way to overcome this "contagion of nothingness"—that swears it loves us, wants only to spare us further disgrace and keep us safe from harm, while incessantly gathering evidence of our loathsomeness—was to create a larger and more imposing self-image that believes we're worthy of love and acknowledgment, worthy of existing; that in order to create an opposing, phantom voice, we must fashion out of our hubris, longing, and ingenuity a persona just as perversely lush and compelling, just as stubbornly fervent and comforting as that of the abyss.

Which is why, so often, sitting at my desk on a cold winter morning, staring out the window at the chilled blur of the sky, I find myself hating everything I've ever written, the very sound of my voice, wondering what ever made me believe I had anything of value to say, why anyone would want to read anything I wrote . . . and then, recognizing its voice, the feeling it's steeped in, another voice will start speaking, reminding me that I've written a few good lines, have taught students I'm proud of, enjoy the idea and fact of having started a school that continues despite all my fears, a voice that blends all the voices of all my favorite writers into one affirming, arguing, capricious, and boisterous testimony that can be heard above all the other's objections.

Why I always knew what to call this dark voice, maybe even especially when I didn't want to acknowledge that I knew: the shit-bird. And why, well over thirty years ago now, I felt so compelled to turn an idea about personas and masks into a method of writing designed to defeat it.

THE SHITBIRD,
NAMED AND UNNAMED

My friend, Ralph Dickey, first used the word in a letter he wrote to me in 1968. I was living in San Francisco after having left the Iowa Writers' Workshop after only a semester because I believed the world was happening everywhere else, and he was back in Iowa, finishing his degree:

> I've found that when I write alone in my attic, I'm not alone in my attic at all. There are maybe a half-dozen critics, themselves symbols of others, who perch on my shoulder like little shit-birds whispering instructions in my ears. Ralph Dickey can hardly get a word in edgewise. I'm fighting that now that I've recognized it. . . . I've been so afraid to be the person I am truly destined to be. I've been willing to accept all kinds of substitutes, disguises, camouflages. The most attractive one to me, I suppose, is that of a Jew, preferably East European or Russian. I used to say, as a Russian Jewish girl I lusted after once said to me, that I had a Slavic Jewish soul. But that's not who I am. I am a black man.

Yes, Ralph was a Black man, or half-Black man. Possessed of an endearing capacity to agitate, influence, and reduce everything to a discrete series of large and small turbulences that left every-one, including himself, and especially me, exhausted and unrecognizable, he wrote beautiful musical poetry about his being Black and white and so ethereally indecipherable he often felt omnipresent and invisible at the same time. Everyone, especially I, found him brilliant, original, overbearingly modest, and insufferably self-conscious to the point of appearing at times to vanish right before our eyes. It's stunning therefore to realize that I only knew him five years, from when we first met at the University of Iowa's Writers' Workshop in 1967, to 1972, when he killed himself, and that these few years would manage to influence and change so much of my life as a writer, teacher, and man.

I was struggling through my first year of teaching college at Kalamazoo College in Michigan, in 1972, when he used the term again in a phone call. Everything was a struggle then for both of us, as if being young writers of ambition in our twenties was based on a logic so absurd neither of us seemed to understand or know how to manage it. He was calling from Oakland, California, to tell me that Ginger, the woman he lived with, had left, and taken her daughter, Chandra, whom he loved as his own. I asked what I always did when I knew he was in trouble: if he was writing. And he always knew what I was really asking: if he were still invested in advancing with his life, despite all the endless obstacles he and fate seemed to place before him. Sometimes, in order to avoid the question, he'd call late and play one of his original jazz pieces and then hang up without saying a word, letting me know that he still had his music, that he still had something he valued, in case I was worried. When it came to Ralph, I was always worried. We were both twenty-six years old, I his senior by three months, which I believed entitled me to ask prying questions he'd grown to expect. But there was no music this time, no abrupt silences. He simply said that he wasn't writing.

He was entering a program called Primal Scream, he said, one that was supposed to help people in his mental and spiritual state, or so others had told him. Primal Scream? I asked, thinking he was kidding me. Yes, he said, that's what it was called; you gave yourself over to it for two weeks, went to classes, talked to gurus/therapist types, and kept a journal to get in touch with your pain. He reminded me that he had a lot to get in touch with. But it was expensive, he said, he would have to sell most of his things. I strongly objected, maybe too strongly—I didn't want him hanging up on me—and offered to give him money so he wouldn't have to sell his piano. He already had, he said, reminding me that I didn't have any anyway, but thanking me, nonetheless.

It was then that I asked him what I'd asked many times before, if he couldn't just write his way through this; isn't that what writers did, write their way through the pain?

No, he said, he couldn't. Every time he sat down to work a big black bird perched on his shoulder and whispered in his ear that poetry and music wouldn't save him, nothing would, he was who he was, and writing about it would only make him more wretched. Wretchedness, it said, was his lot. He tried not to listen, he told me, but he always did. Sometimes he heard my voice, telling him to keep going, my whole number. But he couldn't, he'd give up and just sit there, suffering in silence. Its argument was too strong.

Which was? I asked.

That essentially, he was worthless, shit, and nothing good would ever come of anything he did.

Why a black bird? I wanted to know.

He didn't know, maybe because he was?

I asked him what he called it.

Shitbird, he said. *My* shitbird.

He sounded almost at peace with himself, if you could call such resignation a kind of peace. I then went through what he called my number, reminding him how much he had going for him, more than anyone I knew, I said, I just wished he could see himself through my eyes, the eyes of everyone who loved and admired him. He already had a subject, a world all his own, everyone at Iowa envied him, wished they owned half as much gift, capacity, I said. So few had that much, or ever would. Then he did what he always did when there wasn't anything left to say. He sighed and said he thought he'd give this program a chance, he had nothing to lose but his anonymity.

His "anonymity," the last word he ever said to me.

Everything seemed to happen quickly after our conversation. There was no follow-up after the program, our mutual friend and mentor, the poet Michael S. Harper, explained, and the pain he got in touch with finally overwhelmed him. Maybe because it was all too painful, I was never sure of all the facts—I accepted what Michael told me, without wanting to know more. What I understood was that he sold nearly everything he had to afford the program and moved in with friends afterward, and was no longer working at whatever job he'd had before (there were a number of them in a few years) and now, broke, exhausted, and demoralized, he swallowed slug poison and suffocated himself with a plastic laundry bag in the back seat of the one thing he still apparently owned, his old VW Bug. He did this at the cliffs overlooking San Francisco, the place I first took him to after he followed me out west from Iowa. His white mother, Harper said, dominated the dream journal he kept at the program, a copy of which he sent me. I already knew most of the story but not the emotional depths he connected to in the journal. Ralph was so fair skinned as a child his white father, who believed Ralph was his biological son, didn't realize he wasn't his child until he was six or seven, when his hair started getting curly and his skin darkened to cinnamon. It was then that his mother told him his father wasn't really his father and didn't want him living with them anymore; his real father was a Black man she'd met in a bar one night and never saw again. Which is why he had to go live in a foster home; either he left, or they all had to, she, his white half-brother and sister, and Ralph, too. She told him it was best all around if Ralph didn't live with them anymore, he wrote in his journal, she loved him, she said, and maybe one day he would understand. What he understood, he once told me, was that he wasn't who he thought he was, he wasn't a white boy, he was a Black boy and that's why all these terrible things were happening to him.

After living with a number of foster parents, some abusive, a music teacher, a Black woman who prized him, took him in as a teenager, teaching him to play the piano and providing him with the only stability he ever knew. His love of music led to poetry, but the fact that he kept falling for women who eventually left him only added to his grief. He certainly wouldn't understand why, after all this time, I was now writing about him again, or giving him credit, and responsibility, because of something he said to me during his brief and unsustainable life, that inspired an idea that would preoccupy me for much of my own. I don't remember his ever wanting credit for anything other than the poetry and music he made, if even that. Everything else, he always seemed to be thinking, was just too exhausting, and emotionally depleting.

Every artist is on intimate terms with the allures of the abyss; we all do battle in our own unique, perplexing ways. But few of us ever are required to live in it, to make it our permanent residence. I don't doubt that this shitbird, his dark emblem of irrelevance and decay, came to respect the fight he made to overcome it. Only now do I understand what my great attraction to Ralph was really about. I always thought it had to do with my struggle to save him, and my guilt at having failed. But that's not what it was. It was his great struggle to save himself that so captivated me, and everyone else. The relentlessness of his struggle to overcome the comforts of his abyss.

This is the title poem of the book of Ralph's poetry that Harper published after his death.

LEAVING EDEN

Named and unnamed and renamed
armed and unarmed and disarmed
I have my covenant outside the womb
in the solitary confinement of my cells

The cries of my bones
like the cries of animals
follow me out of my mother
into exile

In Viktor Frankl's examination of life in Auschwitz, *Man's Search for Meaning*, he quotes Dostoyevsky: "There is only one thing that I dread: not to be worthy of my sufferings." The one remnant of dignity, Frankl says, in such a place, is one's ability to choose how to respond to one's fate, no matter how dire. In the copy of the coroner's report that Harper sent me "is a description of said deceased: Age: 27 years, height: 5'9" 107 lbs. grey eyes-black hair." Yes, 107 lbs. The state of perpetual unworthiness and defeat and exile he lived in, even from his own body, had a name. He called it his shitbird. It was more merciless and perverse in its persuasion than a simple death wish; its object was to render him powerless to overcome it. In Ralph's case, there was little comfort there, just the abyss itself. The spell it cast covered every aspect of his life, but for as long as I knew him, he fought it with all his strength and talent, with his poetry and music, with his love of what Keats called truth and beauty—"Beauty is truth, truth beauty,—that is all / Ye know on earth, and all ye need to know"—yes, in his great poem "Ode on a Grecian Urn," Keats plainly stated his goals in poetry, in art, that sustained him for his brief, impassioned life, and that's exactly what sustained Ralph, too: his passion to turn the truth of his pain into something beautiful, lasting. Ralph, indeed, was worthy of his suffering.

I NEVER WANTED TO BE ME,
I DON'T THINK

"Very educational!" I once overheard Allen Ginsberg telling a poet who'd just finished reading poems that were, well, somewhat overburdened with literary allusion. It was the mid-Sixties in a coffeehouse in Haight-Ashbury and the poet was walking past Ginsberg on his way to the counter and everyone there, especially the poet who'd just read, knew what Ginsberg in his inimitable way was saying: poetry served many functions, but educating people isn't, shouldn't be, one of them. Inspire, stimulate, illuminate, disrupt, upset, shake awake maybe, but not educate. Being a poet can be a risky, certainly unconventional, and even dangerous way of life, given that poets often ask themselves to tolerate extreme emotional feelings, and Ginsberg was accusing this poet of hiding behind a safe and phony mask, of being too mundane and cautious to be genuine or profound. When I ran into this poet a few years later, he was still upset. Coming from anyone else he would've shrugged it off, he told me, but having his work and, in a sense, his persona, deemed phony by the kingmaker of masks devastated him.

Ginsberg, whether wearing his Whitmanian mask and addressing all of America in his poem "America" or dealing with his mother's mental illness in "Kaddish" with Ray Charles's blues rhythms and the prophetic pronouncements of the Hebrew anthem, loved playing the many roles of ringmaster, lion tamer, and clown par excellence. As William Carlos Williams put it in his introduction to *Howl*, "This poet sees through and all around the horrors he partakes of. . . . He avoids nothing but experiences to the hilt. He contains it." I met him several times in San Francisco in the Sixties and each time I met a very different man. It'd be easy to say he was always on, performing any role he deemed necessary at the moment, but it was more than that. His larger-than-life Whitmanian persona demanded that he not only overcome his abyss but subject it to every obstacle and whim of his imagination, both in his life and poetry; the performance was all-consuming. The little Jewish boy in Brooklyn seldom got a word in edgewise; there was always too much riding on his thought and idea, as if his every other utterance was a proclamation for the ages.

An example of this is the time he approached me at a cocktail party in New York City in the mid-1980s. He was now a professor of English at Brooklyn College, dressed appropriately in a sport jacket and tie, and I was talking to two of my colleagues from NYU, where I now ran the graduate creative writing program. Sizing up the crowd, he began to talk like a fellow professor until something happened, in his mind at least, and suddenly the poet who'd written "Kaddish" was describing a dream he had the night before, in which his mother, Naomi, appeared at the foot of his bed, holding her decapitated head in her left hand, the head proclaiming in a voice he now imitated in something of a screech for the entire room to hear: "There, rest. No more suffering for you. I know where you've gone, it's good." Lines from his poem "Kaddish," I thought, about forgiveness of guilt and shame. He then smiled, sighed deeply, patted my shoulder, and, quickly muttering something about our discussing his teaching at NYU, turned and left as abruptly as he'd arrived.

"Was that a job interview?" one of my colleagues asked.

It was a performance as unforgettable as any I'd ever witnessed. The voice coming out of Ginsberg's dead mother's mouth sounded a little like William Burroughs, which only made it all the more bizarre, and mesmerizing. No one there uttered another word; we were all lost in a state best described by Williams in the same introduction: "Hold back the edges of your gowns, Ladies, we are going through hell."

Oscar Wilde certainly was onto something when he said, "Man is least himself when he talks in his own person. Give him a mask, and he will tell you the truth." We all design masks behind which we hide our imperfections, the parts of us we deem unworthy of public display. For many, writing is a means of creating an aura of strength and invulnerability, of persuading others that we're worthy of their respect. The kids in my neighborhood in Rochester, New York, in the Fifties, were all from first- and second-generation homes; their parents and grandparents were from Russia, Czechoslovakia, Hungary, Poland, Italy, Ireland, and Ukraine, and we were all, every one of us, kids and adults alike, desperate to be seen as tougher, smarter, of a higher class, anything other than how we saw ourselves reflected in our immigrant families and one another: nobodies lost somewhere between where we came from and where we wanted to go. While in grade school many of us lived on the streets, a world that, however unpredictable and unsafe, was at least familiar and often less unhappy than that of our houses. The masks we all hid behind were designed to win approval, to convince one another and ourselves that we were worthy of respect. We all knew our roles from the movies, comic books, and stories our fathers told (those of us who had one around), roles based on tough guys, braggarts, and big shots of all kinds, loud, shiny, funny stories about troublemakers who were always defying the odds and making themselves the center of everyone's attention. And sometimes these roles became confusing, even dangerous. All summer long I was one of the neighborhood kids playing street games with lamp poles, fire hydrants, and cut-off trashcans used as basketball hoops, and then in the fall these same kids who had only days before been my friends and teammates were suddenly at my front gate wanting to beat me up, because I was the only Jewish kid they knew and the ones who went to Catholic school had been told the Jews killed Christ and they thought they should do something about it.

It didn't have to make sense; fighting became just another game we played, no more or less scary or personal than any other. In the summers we were buddies, and in the fall, sworn enemies. Like it or not, we all lived according to the roles we owned and valued, and when our roles changed, we changed with them. I still carry the scars of one of these "roles" on the palm and thumb of my right hand. It was a game of chicken I invented to show everyone I, a Jew, was as tough and mean as anyone else. One of us would stand on either side of a garage window that swung both ways, each of us taking turns swinging the window at the other's face. The first to duck or step away lost, the trick being to catch the window just before it hit you in the face. It was that simple and brutal, and without doubt this kind of recklessness got me into all kinds of trouble as a kid and later in life, but it most likely also in some ways helped me as a writer in taking on loud bold personas, like Hemingway's and Isaac Babel's, and in pursuing themes as desperate and painful as my father's death, which I interpreted as a suicide and not a heart attack as everyone else saw it as being. To a certain extent, I just didn't seem to care if I got hit by the window or not, which made me, essentially, unbeatable. I must've cared, of course, but, like my father, I refused to show fear. With his chest sucked up and chin thrust forward, à la James Cagney and Humphrey Bogart, my father was always daring the world to take a swing at him, just once.

And one day, after I'd won a game, Tommy Hildebrand, a big dumb hapless kid who almost always lost, swung the window back at me when I wasn't looking. I saw it coming out of the corner of my eye and blocked it with my right hand and all I remember after that was sitting in the back of Tommy's older brother's big red Chevy pickup with a towel wrapped around my hand, watching drops of my blood fly over my head as we drove as fast as I'd ever gone to the hospital on Hudson Avenue, two miles away. And there, being stitched up (twenty-six stitches I can still feel going in and out of my palm and the base of my thumb), by a young doctor who kept telling me how lucky I was that no nerves had been severed, how lucky and what a tough kid I was because I wasn't crying. "I'd be crying my head off in your place," he kept saying. But Alan Ladd or John Wayne wouldn't cry while being stitched up, certainly not Cagney or Edward G. Robinson in *Key Largo* or *Little Caesar*. What I was thinking about was the only time I saw my father cry, and then just heard him through his closed bedroom door. I was seven when he came home early from work and went into their bedroom without saying a word and slammed the door. My mother ran in after him and kept asking him what was wrong and he wouldn't tell her, he just kept making a wheezing noise like he was trying not to sneeze or throw up. I sat outside their door, trying to imagine what terrible thing had happened, and then he was telling her, and she started crying and I did, too, because it was just too awful. He'd seen a little girl, no more than four or five, run into the street and get hit by an ice-cream truck, he said, it happened right in front of him off Rauber Street, which wasn't far away, and he didn't think she could survive, she was still under the truck when the ambulance and police came. He was making the sucking sound, only louder now, and my mother was telling him something I couldn't hear. He just couldn't stop thinking about it, he said, crying louder now, seeing it happen over and over again without being able to do anything. Which is why I wasn't crying then, while being stitched up, because that was so much worse than a few stitches. I never saw him cry before or after that.

Yes, the mask I sometimes use when I'm beginning a poem dealing with something difficult is the face my father wore when I was fourteen and we drove around on weekends looking for new locations for his vending machines. He worked nights as a janitor at Kodak to make money to buy candy and peanut machines to put in pool halls and gas stations and sometimes on weekends we'd drive around looking for larger locations to get his new vending business started. "Just one or two little candy machines here or there," he'd say to any big shot he could find on a factory floor at Fashion Park Clothing or DuPont's, "what harm can it do?" I'd sit beside him in our old Ford station wagon (the rust-bucket, we called it) in a factory parking lot, watching him transform himself from a little schlep in baggy clothes covered in coffee dust and powdered cream into someone the "big shots would listen to." It was quite a show, and sometimes he'd talk out loud to some imaginary big shot, telling him how much his employees would enjoy a Mounds bar and cup of cocoa during a break. Whispering to the rearview mirror, making weird guttural sounds and swallowing what I imagined was a good portion of his fear, he wouldn't even remember I was there, sitting right next to him, he was so intent on selling this imaginary man something only he could sell.

Then I'd follow him through a back door and up stairways and down shiny hallways until he found someone in a suit who looked important and he'd immediately go into his song-and-dance routine, mixing Borscht Belt humor with equal amounts of connivance and artful salesman persuasion. At first the big shot would look at him as if wondering how he got in the building, but then would suddenly start laughing and call another big shot over and before long we'd drive away with a new location. When we went to service his machines the bosses and workers alike would all come running to see the show, and get free cups of coffee and Mars bars, and none of this was wasted on me. I learned from a master salesman. Years before I published my first poetry collection, *Like Wings*, in 1978, and was new to the city, I kept dropping by the NYU English department until I finally got its secretary to give me an appointment with the chairman. She wasn't easy to convince but my persistence finally paid off and the chairman later joked that the only reason he agreed to see me was because he wanted to meet the guy who'd managed to charm his secretary, he hadn't thought it possible. The appointment led to one creative writing class, an adjunct position, which eventually became a full-time appointment and a graduate writing program. I was doing what came naturally, selling myself before I had anything like a book or career to sell. Writing, certainly, is a kind of salesmanship in which the reader is being convinced that what they're reading is worth their time. Dad was always selling himself, while in writing I'm often selling an idea about trust, sympathy, and how I want to be perceived.

Often enough, though, when using a persona in my work, I seem to experience a feeling of having been displaced without my permission by a facsimile of myself I can't quite recognize, a not unfamiliar, troubling sense of feeling lost and inconclusive; the sense that perhaps there is no real me. In a recent poem, I found myself so perplexed by the lines "I never wanted to be me, / I don't think" I kept cutting them out and then replacing them. I just couldn't understand why I would say something so helpless and off-putting out loud, did I want people, strangers, to think that I didn't like myself? Well, sometimes I didn't, certainly, but why would I confess publicly to such painful ambivalence? Was this simply the voice of my shitbird or was it that of a persona more honestly attuned to my feelings of vulnerability and confusion? Knowing the difference is usually something of a dilemma. I could almost hear the voice of the ten-year-old me arguing not to reveal any weakness of character to the tough kids waiting at the front gate to beat him up. But the poet in me knows that vulnerability and fear can also be experienced as inspiration and excitement, sometimes even a kind of ecstasy. Eventually, despite the discomfort it caused, I decided to keep the lines knowing that I often feel tentative while writing. Indeed, in its black-and-white world, the shitbird sees self-exploration as threatening and confession a kind of persecution. Self-devaluation and camouflage are its religion, its means of survival, which, of course, renders the creative process its mortal enemy.

These lines appears in a poem, "The Difference Between," from my most recent collection of poems, *Luxury*.

> Something vibrant and shiny
> is always hurrying away from me,
> some kind of possibility
> of fidelity to what, and whom,
> I meant to be. Something
> vaguely necessary, even essential.
> The difference between
> being late and early,
> open and closed, bereft
> and on the verge

of something more interesting.
An opulent refrain, say,
trying to maintain,
and keep up with what's vanishing
around the corner from
where I stand, waiting
to be a little less solemn
and arcane,
a little more concrete. Someone
possessed of a quality
one can acknowledge,
even forgive. In any case,
there I am, remain,
a thought leaning
just out of reach,
glistening like a fish
at the back of my psyche,
infused
with vibrant possibility.
Is this why I remain
faithful to everything
I've lost along the way?
I never wanted to be me,
I don't think. Once
a beguiling idea
disguised as a question
to which no answer
exists.

It's this use of a borrowed and stitched-together persona that so often speaks for me when I write, this notion that one can fashion out of one's longing and despondency an identity confident, straightforward, and expectant enough to reveal its own source of loneliness and confusion without betraying or lessening itself, a presence formidable enough to impress maybe even Allen Ginsberg himself.

PITY AND FEAR

Walker Percy's novel *The Moviegoer* was the first novel I read straight through. I was sixteen and in a Woolworth's store in a shopping mall outside Rochester, waiting for my mother to finish getting her hair done in a nearby salon at the mall, when, not knowing what else to do, I began looking at books in a revolving kiosk next to the cashier aisle. I then became interested in one with a black-and-white cover in which the boxed views of a man's perplexed face made it seem as if he was arguing with himself. The warm words of praise on the back cover made me imagine people saying things like that about me, and no sooner had I glanced at the first page than I found myself enthralled by the warm, charming voice of its first-person persona narrator, Binx Bolling, who seemed to be talking directly to me. The intimacy of this voice made me feel that I alone was smart and perceptive enough to understand what he was telling me, a secret so essential that only the two of us could possibly understand. I didn't have many friends, none that I could talk to the way this writer was talking to me, and that alone was enough to make me pony up the $1.95 price, even though I could have checked it out of the library.

The novel was about things I liked, or wanted to do, like going to movies and riding through the countryside in a sports car with pretty women, but there were other darker philosophical things too, about very serious things like despair and verification, things I was drawn to but wouldn't fully understand until I reread the book many years later. Though none of that mattered then. What mattered was the sad, wistful voice of the narrator that made me feel I was eavesdropping on a private conversation I was having with myself. It was the voice I used when I was frightened and lonely and needed to believe that I wasn't entirely alone, that made me feel purposeful and valued. The quiet, confident way Binx listed things he liked to do after work made these simple things seem almost magical, if not essential: "It is my custom on summer evenings after work to take a shower, put on shirt and pants and stroll over to the deserted playground and there sit on the ocean wave, spread out the movie page of the *Times-Picayune* on one side, phone book on the other, and a city map in my lap. After I have made my choice, plotted a route—often to some remote neighborhood like Algiers or St. Bernard—I stroll around the schoolyard in the last golden light of day and admire the building. . . . It gives me a pleasant sense of the goodness of creation to think of the brick and the glass and the aluminum being extracted from such common dirt . . ."

I cried when I finished the book that first time, and not because I didn't want it to end—I wanted every book I read to end as quickly as possible due to my anxiety with reading; I cried because I didn't want Binx to stop talking to me, to stop being my friend. Nothing else, not even a book of van Gogh's paintings that I stole from a downtown department store, made me feel that special. I didn't steal a lot of things as some kids I knew did, only those things I especially valued, and I very much wanted this book, and not having any money, stealing it was the only way I could own it. The fact that I got caught and my father had to come to the store to pay for it didn't make me love the pictures any less; in fact, it made me treasure them even more. I didn't understand how emotionally expensive these paintings were to paint, or anything about van Gogh himself, but I did understand on some secret level that the humiliation I suffered in getting the book bore some relationship to the paintings themselves; that suffering had something to do with the ecstasy it created.

On its surface the story of *The Moviegoer* is simple: Binx is ordered by his great aunt to "help" his distant cousin Kate, fearing she will harm herself after her fiancé has died, which he attempts to do and, in the process, finds a way out of the "everydayness" of his own despair. "To be aware of the possibility of the search is to be onto something. Not to be onto something is to be in despair," Binx tells us. It's Binx's search I so powerfully identified with, his need to find an identity greater than himself, an identity not unlike those of his movie heroes, which no doubt is what I wanted too. My uncle Jake, who lived in the small room off our kitchen, listening to a police radio all night, was a stagehand at the Paramount movie house in downtown Rochester. All I had to do was knock three times on a back-alley door and he'd let me in for free. I knocked three times once or twice a week all through grade school and much of high school, always sitting in the same balcony seat to the left of the screen, where I could see Jake high up in his nest near the ceiling, opening and closing the curtains to end and begin what for each of us must've been hours spent among the only friends we had, the phantom images that seemed to play inside and outside our heads in dreamlike sequences we valued above all others. Long before I began to read and value books, I understood what Binx meant when he said he wanted something more than the "every-dayness" of his life. He wanted what I wanted, to feel important to myself, not ordinary and forgettable. He seemed to be giving me permission to be myself, to want more than the immigrant kids around me wanted, permission to feel ambitious and special. It didn't matter that I read so slowly, often painfully; suddenly the idea of becoming a writer like Percy became a kind of sanctuary, a nest high and away from everything else, a personal quest for meaning and escape. I wanted to make people feel the way he made me feel, important enough to be spoken to with purpose, and intelligence.

One passage particularly moved me. Binx is walking through the French Quarter of New Orleans and becomes interested in an unhappy-looking young college-aged couple walking just ahead. Assuming they're newlyweds on their honeymoon like so many others there, he imagines that the young man is unhappy because he fears all the other young men, also on their honeymoons, are more worldly and exotic and, compared to them, he must appear ordinary in his bride's eyes. His bride is unhappy, Binx thinks, because the young man is, and because she has no idea why. The young man, Binx thinks, is being consumed by his everydayness, which renders him invisible, and superfluous. Binx then spots the famous actor William Holden strolling just ahead, his movie-star stature casting a glow over everything around him, including the unhappy couple. When a group of middle-aged women Holden stops to ask for a match become flustered, the young man sees his opportunity and saunters up nonchalantly and lights Holden's cigarette, and then he, Holden, and his bride all walk off together, chatting amiably. It's Holden's "peculiar reality" that fascinates Binx, the special aura of those engaged in a search to overcome the malaise of the ordinary, Cioran's "contagion of nothingness," and the boy's and now mine, too. It wasn't Holden's celebrity or the boy's enthrallment and moment of self-possession that so mesmerized me, but Percy's capacity to show the reader (me) a way to proceed by allowing me to look at the world through Binx's more philosophically sophisticated eyes.

The novel was inspirational. I wanted to do exactly what Percy was doing: to create first-person narrators who spoke with authority and intimacy, who helped others recognize and embrace whatever small sense of the sublime they were capable of. I wanted to see the world from a more gracious and philosophical perspective, the way Binx did, to adapt his fictional persona for myself. I was suddenly on a search of my own, for my own personas that might capture similar particular states of mind and feelings, a search that continues even now. Through high school and into college I found many personas to emulate in the poems and texts I loved: James Wright's vulnerably wholehearted and earnest narrator in *The Branch Will Not Break*, Theodore Roethke's narrator's joyous grief and celebration of nature in "The Lost Son," Hemingway's Jake Barnes's reconciliation with his own sexual despair in *The Sun Also Rises*, Elizabeth Bishop's clear-eyed negotiation with youthful consciousness in "The Waiting Room" and "The Moose," and especially George Konrád's social worker for neglected and orphaned children in *The Case Worker* who, in his own mind, is "a radioactive *tableau vivant* gashed by light." These writers and their personas seemed to understand me better than I understood myself; their investigation and search into the mystifying nature of their suffering was exactly what I wanted to do in my own writing.

This quote from an essay on Aristotle by Joe Sachs in the Internet Encyclopedia of Philosophy pretty much sums up the power of persuasion that Walker had over me, enough so to make me want to do what he did for the rest of my life.

> *The five marks of tragedy that we learned of from Aristotle's* Poetics—*that it imitates an action, arouses pity and fear, displays the human image as such, ends in wonder, and is inherently beautiful—give a true and powerful account of the tragic pleasure.*

My persona method of writing is all about imitation as a means of arousing pity and fear in the service of providing wonder and beauty, though I most certainly didn't know that until recently when I read Sachs's essay on Aristotle, who believed the purpose of tragedy is to permit catharsis to take place.

Aristotle would disagree with Ginsberg—he believed writing is, in a sense, educational, the art of providing knowledge, and therefore elucidation, sustenance, and ultimately, satisfaction; knowledge leads to wisdom. This is what we writers must ask of ourselves, to turn our pity and fear into understanding and satisfaction. Is this why my friend Ralph Dickey wrote about what it feels like to grow up in a world that didn't seem to want anything to do with him, what it felt like to find inspiration in the seclusion of his imagination? Why Theodore Roethke wrote about his seizures, which he would suffer sometimes in public while teaching, and about his fear of losing his mind, in poems like "In a Dark Time": "What's madness but nobility of soul / at odds with circumstance?" In the mid-Sixties I took a poetry class with the poet Jack Gilbert at San Francisco State College and I never forgot the story he told about how Roethke suffered a seizure while teaching and, struggling to maintain his dignity before his students, continued reciting whatever poem he was teaching even while being placed in a straitjacket and carried out to an ambulance. Gilbert's point was the "nobility of soul" Roethke insisted on demonstrating in the midst of great suffering, and then later, in the act of writing about it, creating for himself and the reader the kind of profound satisfaction found only in beautifully made objects.

In George Konrád's superb first novel, *The Case Worker*, his first-person narrator explains his job trying to help his hopeless clients in a Hungarian welfare building: "Suicides have been giving me a lot of work lately. Abandoning home, hearth, and work, they plunge into the silence that knows no suffering. They depart in haste, mysteriously, as though to take the long trip. . . . Of all nations mine has the highest suicide rate. Does that make it the freest?" Perhaps because I too worked in a welfare building in San Francisco in the late Sixties and could identify with the great sympathy Konrád showed toward "the silence that knows no suffering," and knew firsthand the horror he was writing about with such vision and perspicacity, I was especially influenced both as a writer and as a citizen of another nation with a high suicide rate. There is certainly a great deal of pity and fear to be found in this book, and, as a consequence, as much catharsis as one can bear.

And there is perhaps no better example of the use of catharsis than in Elizabeth Bishop's poem about inconceivable loss, "One Art," in which she deals with the suicide of her longtime Brazilian lover, Lota de Macedo Soares, in 1967. In comparing this kind of loss with the idea of losing things in general, she not only creates the perfect metaphor for loss, but underplays what for her is a great tragedy with losing "some realms I owned, rivers, even a continent," things she missed that are ultimately no "disaster." In fact, the more she undercuts the idea of disaster the more the word takes on its solemn register of tragic consequence. In this list of what is lost in losing her great friend, there is not only great pity and fear but a great tension that builds to catharsis in the last two lines of the final stanza: "the art of losing's not too hard to master / though it may look like (*Write* it!) like disaster."

Another example is an early poem I wrote, "Gogol's Coat," that also deals with loss, in this case, loss of love. I based it on Gogol's great short story "The Overcoat," in which a lowly clerk loses his most prized possession, a new overcoat, to thieves. The story ends with his dying of a fever and his ghost retuning to steal the coats of those whose indifference to his suffering Gogol probably saw as a great societal illness. Whatever he was after, it's a story unlike any anyone had written before, one that Dostoyevsky referred to as being seminal to all subsequent Russian fiction: "We have all come from under *The Overcoat*." I used the clerk's great disappointment as a metaphor to describe my own sense of loss and rejection. The poem came quickly, and I remember how surprised I was by its ending, especially the use of the word "forgiven." There was certainly pity and fear here, and for me, at least, catharsis.

GOGOL'S COAT

I mean to imagine the wilderness
where trees are not trees when touched.
The lover's longing when he wakes
with his head on her belly, his hand lost
in that dark. How then most of all
the trees are not trees when touched.

I think of Gogol's clerk whose desire
for a skin so exquisite all Russia's winds
would brush off his chest like a kiss
is the lover's to be inside
where the trees are not trees when touched.

How as he stands before the mirror
& sees himself inside the coat, at last,
the salt of stars on his tongue, he remains
himself the clerk when touched, but loves
the coat which cannot be forgiven.

Whether writers are dealing with grief, great disappointment, or societal horror, we all share the same hope that what we may write next will change or enhance or resolve the source of all our suffering, often enough so that finding in ourselves the very thing we fear and hate inspires our most excruciatingly exquisite possession: our vulnerability.

Yes, this is why, despite my fear that others will see me as weird, absurd, or obscene, I insist on pursuing so fully-and-semiconsciously, abjectly, and willingly, every creative instinct, adding yet another rumor, whisper, image, or anecdote to this ongoing, illicit, often preposterously precious spilling of the beans; that despite the little black bird perched on my shoulder, reminding me constantly of the thousand and one reasons to remain silent, when my desire to create is greater than my fear, I find the strength to pursue the truth about whatever it is I truly feel under all my lies and obfuscations, and then know how to proceed. And that even when the fear is too great and I stop and never want to write again, it isn't a lack of strength or will that has stopped me, or a matter of fault or blame. It is the comforts of the abyss that have stopped me, the lies and convenient truths that hide just below the level of my consciousness, behind which I seek refuge and blindness. And even if I can go no further, I now know something about myself that I wouldn't have attained any other way, something that will help me with future projects.

But for those of us who persist there is the satisfaction of having successfully restructured some previously unassailable aspect of our emotional landscape into something presentable, something that "arouses pity and fear . . . that ends in wonder, and is inherently beautiful," the reward being the kind of emotional truth that will afford us the perspective with which to view ourselves in an entirely new and more enlightened and even kinder way, despite all our fears and misgivings, and the endless equivocations of our big black birds.

MY TWO LIBRARIES

There are any number of reasons I'll never forget the Saturday morning in 1961 the day after Ernest Hemingway killed himself. For one thing, news of his suicide was everywhere, on TV and radio and in all three Rochester newspapers and my father was arguing with my uncle Jake in the kitchen while Jake was eating, about the reasons Hemingway did it. None of us, not my father, my mother, me, or even my grandma, his mother, who fed him, ever went anywhere near him when he was eating and slurping his endless courses of wiener schnitzels, soups, kugels, sauerkrauts, and flavored seltzers spread out over the kitchen table like migratory birds just waiting to take off and never see any of us again. In fact, no one, including any of our neighbors, ever wanted to go near him for any reason under any conditions. He paid all the bills while my father was always trying to get one of his businesses off the ground, which is why we watched TV and even read in the dark, because he went around turning off the lights, yelling about the cost of electricity, daring any of us to turn a light on in his presence. Which certainly has a lot to do with why my mother got only one shelf in the icebox and we ate in diners three or four nights a week.

And there they were, Jake and my father, together in the kitchen at the same time, with all the lights on and everyone else standing around listening to them argue about all the reasons they thought

Hemingway had killed himself. I was sixteen, impatient to go off with my father and help him fill his vending machines and then have some time to myself, but also truly amazed that my father was breaking all his own rules about avoiding Jake at every opportunity. All he seemed to care about was building up his vending business so we could finally move out and get our own house and get away from Jake. Everybody who ever met Jake wanted the same thing: to get away from him as quickly as possible.

Maybe, my father was shouting, maybe someone else killed Hemingway, why would someone so rich and famous blow his own brains out. It wasn't all that surprising, Jake yelled back, Hemingway wasn't writing anything good, was alcoholic, depressed, and just had electroshock therapy after walking into a running airplane propeller. But he had all those houses, women, and movies made from his books, my father shouted back even louder, who in his right mind would want to die with all that success?

That was his point, Jake screamed: HE WASN'T IN HIS RIGHT MIND GODDAMMIT!

We'd read two of Hemingway's Nick Adam stories the previous spring in my tenth grade English class, and I was remembering that my teacher, Mrs. Harper, said that Hemingway's father had also killed himself, and the same way, with a gun, and I was thinking about maybe mentioning that, but my mother kept looking at me the way she did when she didn't want me to make any trouble, so I just stood there, waiting for them to wind down. One thing was clear to all of us, even my grandmother, who was standing by the front door in case she needed to make a quick getaway: only one of them knew what he was talking about and it wasn't my father, who'd probably never read a book in his life. I had never seen him read anything, not even a newspaper, because he was probably dyslexic like me and also didn't know it. In fact, there was very little any of us knew about anything, but we all did know that Jake had literary ambitions, which is why he was always staying up all night writing letters to newspaper editors, and getting them published too. But most of all, there were all those boxes of fancy literary books up in the attic that, starting when I was twelve, I'd sneak up there to look at. All the first editions of Hemingway's *The Sun Also Rises*, Ezra Pound's *Personae* and *Poems 1918–21*, William Butler Yeats's *A Packet for Ezra Pound*, handprinted by his own Cuala Press, *Literary Essays* by Mark Twain, and *Sons and Lovers* by D. H. Lawrence, plus boxes of literary journals like *Hound and Horn* and Ford Madox Ford's *The Transatlantic Review*, in which, because it was where Hemingway published, I published my first short story while in graduate school—all of which he kept in a small room at the front of our attic. It didn't seem to matter that I still wasn't much of a reader yet, I knew they were special because of the way they were covered in cellophane and in boxes covered in blankets, and their fancy paper and print and the way the sentences looked so refined, as if all these writers cared how each one looked and sounded, even in dusty attics in crummy old houses like ours. And this was long before I read Walker Percy and began to see myself as a reader, let alone a writer.

But what made all this even more exciting, and maybe even a little dangerous, was the fact that in a smaller room at the back of the attic was Jake's other library: boxes of old and new copies of *Playboy*, *Swank*, *Gala*, *Naked in Nature*, *Esquire*, and countless photos of naked women. Dangerous because the only door to the attic was in Jake's room and I was always listening for his footsteps on the stairs. All of which in some way made every minute I spent going from one room to the other not only shameful but, in a way I didn't understand, transcendent. It was as if I were hobnobbing with the very people Jake could only dream about knowing, the only people I thought he truly admired: intelligent, creative, accomplished writers who earned their keep by using their minds and literary instincts, the kind he wished he could be. The kind I maybe had some small chance to be counted among. Even then I understood it was the one unforgivable thing I could do: be what he dreamed about being and couldn't. He was always bragging about the writers he wrote letters to, never mentioning hearing anything back. And when one of my cartoons—I was my high school's cartoonist—got reprinted in the *Times Union*, our evening newspaper, and my mother was bragging about it to a neighbor, Jake came bursting out of his room, screaming about what a little genius I was, it didn't matter that I didn't learn to read till I was in the fifth grade and got held back twice, I was a real little genius. This was only one of many things I knew I would never forgive him for.

After he left for work, I would go through his room, knowing I was trespassing and that he'd go nuts and never stop screaming if he caught me. His room itself was something of a marvel of technical weirdness, with everything suspended on wires from his ceiling—pens, scissors, even his TV and police radio on shelves suspended on wires—his books and magazines piled up on his bed (which was maybe the only thing in the room not suspended on wires) so he could barely move when he was in it, and photos of famous directors and actors, like George Cukor and Eddie Cantor, whom he'd been a stagehand for when they brought shows to Rochester, all over the walls and ceiling (yes, ceiling!). And then I would feel a little suspended on wires myself between these two very different attic libraries, which, different as they were, seemed to offer me in a way I didn't yet understand two provocative means of storytelling: one purely exhibitionist and the other more refined. Both were also seductively forbidden and illicit, one offering the secrets of the body and the other of the mind, each in its own way representing a choice between the very things I would later come to understand as the precincts of the abyss: shame and fear, satisfaction and pleasure. From my early teens to the time I turned eighteen and my father died of a heart attack at the end of my senior year of high school, I'd go from one of Jake's rooms to the other, visiting what seemed two aspects of a world only Jake himself could husband. In a sense, he was my first librarian, a librarian who also served as a stand-in for my shitbird.

Yes, Jake, who walked two and a half miles to work every day because he'd started so many fights on city buses none of the drivers would stop for him; who screamed and pounded on the locked bathroom door as my mother, my grandma, and I hid inside until he wore himself out; who, as an army psychiatrist once told my mother after Jake came home from WWII, which he'd fought mostly on an army base in Texas with other American soldiers, was the kind of paranoid schizophrenic who wasn't institutionalized only because he could wash, dress himself, and keep a job—yes, Jake, who in his own inimitable way managed to offer me not only my early education as a writer but my first intimation of the comforts of the abyss.

And it was also during this unforgettable argument about Hemingway that my mother, who almost never said anything she didn't absolutely have to, opened her mouth and said, "Maybe he just wanted to stop being miserable—money and being famous isn't happiness, regardless of what you both think."

We all looked at her, even Grandma, who always avoided looking at anyone for too long, because that's when the Evil Eye started to work its magic. And the expression on my mother's face was another thing about that morning that I'll never forget. She was angry, for one thing, angry enough to allow her to show us all just how much smarter she was than any of the rest of us, certainly than my father and Jake. Smarter and much more intuitive. Her contempt was obvious and justified. It was the same expression she had the day I visited her many years later in the state-run apartment complex where she lived for about ten or so years before she got Alzheimer's and had to be moved into a dementia ward at a Jewish Home, where she died. My father and Jake were both dead, and I finally found the courage to ask her something I'd wondered about for most of my life: why she ever married my father to begin with, someone who seemed to offer her nothing but endless heartache and disappointment. It was the same look of dismay and stupefaction, before it quickly turned to anger. The reason was, she said, growing angrier as she spoke, because, knowing how much she wanted to get away from Jake and her mother, from all her crazy neighbors and her job as a filing clerk at a department store downtown, he promised her she could leave her job, and they would move into a house in the suburbs. She was thirty-two, which was old for a woman in those days to get married and have children, and she was desperate to have a family and begin her new life, she said. And she not only believed him then, but was dumb enough to believe him when, two weeks before their wedding, he explained how he'd been embezzled by his accountant and lost all his money and would have to move into her mother's house "for just a month or two." She would have to continue working at Neisner's too, just until he got back on his feet, which should only be a few months, maybe a year or so. Then she'd have a big house with a garden and a big backyard where she could entertain all her friends. Well, she said, her hands balled into fists, she kept on believing him after two months became two years and finally twenty years. She just couldn't stand up for herself, she said, smashing her fists against my chest, again and again, as if it was I who had betrayed her. Twenty years of failed businesses and disappointments and she never once opened her mouth and said a word, she cried.

But she was speaking now. And as remarkable as this was, something even more remarkable happened later that Saturday morning when my father and I were driving to one of his vending machine locations. Stopped at a red light, he suddenly turned and looked at me and, using my name, which in itself was remarkable, because he never called me by name and I sometimes wondered if he actually knew what it was, said, "Philip, you read books like his, Hemingway's, in school—what do you think, is Jake right? He did it because he wasn't writing and was unhappy?"

This was the first and only time that I can remember my father ever asking me what I thought about anything. Suddenly, I wasn't the lackluster know-nothing boy who barely got by in school and did strange things like draw and paint pictures, but someone who knew about things so important my father would have to ask me about them, which is what he was doing, admitting there was something I knew more about than he did. And to make sure I sounded like I knew what I was talking about, I used the voice Hemingway used in one of his Nick Adams stories, "Indian Camp," a story about his doctor father delivering a baby in an Indian camp, in which Nick witnesses his father struggling under great duress. It was a voice so direct and clear and full of masculine bravado and helpless angst that I actually remembered it well enough to use it to say, "I don't know for sure, of course, but maybe if Hemingway couldn't write anymore, like Jake said, and it was the only thing he knew how to do well, maybe he wouldn't want to go on living."

He looked at me as if he wasn't sure who I was. "Well, maybe your mother is right," he said more to himself than me, "maybe having everything sometimes isn't enough . . ."

The next day I got a copy of *The Sun Also Rises* out of the library (I didn't want to go anywhere near any of Jake's books now) and stayed up half the night reading it, and then took out *The Old*

Man and the Sea, reading it not the way I read for school but the way I looked at van Gogh's paintings, reading the words over and over again until I could almost taste each syllable and phoneme, each punctuation mark, until I felt I could taste the *meaning* as something alive and vibrant, wanting to absorb it into my very being.

I then started reading this way all the time, during lunch hour and after homework, sometimes during breaks while helping my father, in factory stairwells and empty lunchrooms, reading the way I'd never read before, devouring the music of the dialogue and the abrupt hard surfaces of the ideas. I can't say when I first realized that Hemingway's tough, self-assured narrators reminded me of my father, but they did, in the way they reduced everything, all their beliefs, ideas, and experience, to a simple code of behavior based on success and the shame of failure and cowardice. They both talked a lot about their appetites, as if no one else had any, and they each seemed to believe that everything that happened to them, everything they said and did, was worth everyone's undivided attention. In many ways they couldn't have been more different, of course: my father was an uneducated Russian-Jewish immigrant who didn't speak a word of English when he came to this country as a child of six and, as I said, never read a book that I could see, while Hemingway, born in the refined suburbs of Chicago of educated and worldly parents, was a voracious reader who lived a high-octane literary life. Yes, it was preposterous to compare my father to perhaps the most influential writer of fiction in the last century, but my adolescent mind was doing just that. They both had domineering, powerful mothers and troubled, anxious fathers, were pugilistic and audacious, possessed a grandiose faith in their own powers of originality and autonomy, and were defiantly self-destructive and, ultimately, suicidal; my father knowingly worked himself to death.

It was during my senior year in high school that my father's business began failing and I helped him after school and on weekends, a time when, without my knowing it, I began viewing my life through many of Hemingway's narrators' eyes, through Hemingway's own eyes. Suddenly, magically, my crazy, always outraged uncle Jake, my perversely stubborn, wildly superstitious, and fate-defying, bedeviled grandma, my perpetually despondent and devoted, endlessly self-sacrificing mother and combatively grandiose, peasant-minded father, were all magically transformed into the kind of richly textured characters I read about in Hemingway's stories about fathers and sons, old fighters and soldiers coming home from the war lonely and confused, characters who seemed to believe in something larger and grander than the claustrophobic dishevelment of their immediate lives. They were suddenly characters in fiction, supported by and enlarged with a purpose greater than the meandering happenstance of their small and hopeless lives. And seeing my family, and myself, through this larger, more generous perspective afforded me the endearments of spectacle and enterprise. My family and I myself became characters in a story more meaningful than anything I had imagined before, to the point of appearing almost entertaining, and even enigmatic.

In other words, we all suddenly made a kind of sense, the kind Hemingway made in so large and magnanimous a way. And this more generous view of the world no doubt helped me survive the shock of my father's sudden death, when, feeling begrudging and lost, I now owned a calculus against which I could measure everything else, against even the shame and confusion of death, a persona that combined Hemingway's and my father's bravado and appetite for achievement, that would allow me to realize what I suddenly wanted more than anything else: some modicum of self-respect. I now also knew what I wanted to do in life; I wanted to transform myself into someone who could make people feel the way Hemingway made me feel, the way my father made me feel in the car that Saturday morning when he asked me what I thought about Hemingway, without telling me what he thought first.

WHICH IS WHY IT SEEMED more than a coincidence when, nine years later, while visiting Hemingway's grave in Ketchum, Idaho, I would get to not only see his house and visit with his widow, Mary, but see the room where he killed himself. I was twenty-seven years old and had just finished my first teaching job as a writer-in-residence at Kalamazoo College the previous June and after spending the summer in Taos, New Mexico, writing poems, I decided to drive up to Montana to see Marie, with whom I'd once again broken up the previous spring. She'd written asking if I wouldn't like to see Rollins, Montana, the place where she grew up, and I went up there from Taos knowing that this probably meant we'd get back together again. We'd separated several times before but for a reason neither of us understood we were somehow always a little less lost and in between things when together and still seemed to need each other. The following year we would break up for good, but all that seemed remote during a lovely week visiting with her family and sightseeing in a very beautiful part of the country I never expected to see. When it was good between us, we were very much in love, and getting to see her in the place she came from put everything in perspective, even our often-troubled relationship. She was a backcountry girl, of blond Anglo-Saxon origins, indigenous to a world of mountain lakes, woods, and scant resources and ambitions, while I in many ways was her exact opposite, a first-generation Russian-Polish Jew of some education and ambition; the differences were as vast as they were curious and attractive. We were so vastly different, in fact, that we existed in a constant state of mutual fascination and uncertainty. She was interested in photography, though not in the same way I was passionate about my writing, and this difference became a void between us, and a source of resentment, which, after a time, bred a certain degree of contempt on her part. How dare I already know what I wanted to do with my life, and get degrees and publications and teaching jobs, while she could barely tell people what she was and wanted to be. Her unfaithfulness, I imagined, was her way of demonstrating this contempt. On the other hand, I found the very nature of her unfaithfulness a curiosity that at times seemed to have little to do with me, or our relationship. The fact that we'd somehow managed to spend over a year together in San Francisco, another year in Iowa, where I finished my degree in writing, and another in Kalamazoo, and that we were now heading back east together to Saratoga Springs, New York, where I'd been offered a month's residency at Yaddo, a writers' retreat, and where she would try to find work while I wrote, well, this had to mean something positive, didn't it?

I think we trusted what we each liked and loved about each other, trusted the friendship that grew out of it. And when I decided that Ketchum, Idaho, wasn't too far out of our way and, knowing my love for Hemingway, Marie went along with that, this somehow made us feel all the closer. She was, after all, sharing, if not borrowing, my dream. We had no plans after my stay at Yaddo and didn't seem to particularly care, and, after we visited his grave and had time to kill, this sense of adventure no doubt also led, I suppose, to my getting Hemingway's phone number from information—a gas station attendant told me it was listed—and calling his house. Mary Hemingway, the attendant told us, was a very nice woman and she and two of his granddaughters and their families were also summering there. Marie, I didn't doubt, just assumed I'd do something crazy like that all along. Why would I drive so far out of our way just to visit a grave?

When a woman answered, I, believing I was speaking to her

housekeeper, asked if I could speak to Mrs. Hemingway, and when the woman politely asked why I wanted to speak to her, I said I'd just visited Hemingway's grave and now very much wanted to see his house. I'd driven maybe a thousand miles out of my way and what harm could it do, I added somewhat breathlessly. It was a few hundred miles at most, so I was lying now, but Hemingway, I knew, lied about his war experiences and made up just about everything else about himself, except the truth he put in his writing, all his writing. The fact that she was laughing now was encouraging, and to keep her—I suspected I wasn't talking to a maid now—on the phone I named all the places Marie and I had been to in the past few months, adding the fact that I was Hemingway's second biggest fan and very much wanted to see the house where he'd written much of one of my favorites of his books, *A Moveable Feast*. Laughing loudly now, she then asked if I happened to know who his first biggest fan was, given that I was only the second biggest. Without pausing, I said that I was in fact both the first and second but hadn't wanted to brag. She then introduced herself as Mary Hemingway and gave me directions up to their house, a few miles away.

It was a big handsome two-story house on a hill overlooking a large piece of land that ran along a river and when we drove into her driveway in my old Opal station wagon whose gear shift was held in place with a stick and rope and that was filled to bursting with just about everything we owned in the world, a short attractive middle-aged blonde woman was standing in the doorway smiling, I thought, at the rather delicate condition our car was in. When she said that we apparently didn't travel lightly, I tried to explain that neither of us really knew where or what we were doing next, a comment she appeared to enjoy. So, we were vagabonds, she said, smiling, and then added that since I didn't appear to have any trouble representing myself, she suspected that I was a writer. Yes, I said, I wrote both fiction and poetry and Marie was a photographer and still something of the hippie she was when I first met her in San Francisco two years earlier, "hippie" being a term and description Marie enjoyed. We followed her inside and after a brief tour of the house, sat with her on a patio looking out over the surrounding fields and spectacular mountains. She was impressed, she said, that we had gone so far out of our way to visit her late husband's grave; Ketchum, she pointed out, wasn't exactly on the way east from Rollins, Montana. And then she said Hemingway would've been intrigued by the fact that I wrote poetry as well as fiction, he enjoyed referring to himself as a failed poet and when I tried to explain my fascination with her late husband, mentioning in passing that I not only owned a first edition of *The Sun Also Rises* but had it in my car, traveling with all the books I cared to keep, she asked to see it. I quickly found it in a carefully packaged box, and she seemed truly amazed to see this rather fragile original Scribner's edition with the pasted-on labels, a copy of which she herself didn't own, she said, and then asked how I came by it. I explained about my crazy uncle Jake's two libraries and she clapped her hands and laughed for a long time, and then asked what other books he had and if I just carried them with me wherever I went. Some of my books I'd left back in Kalamazoo but I had all the ones I cared about with me, like the Yeats and Ezra Pound volumes. You are both truly itinerant, she said, and then talked about how much she and Ernest loved it up here in the mountains, away from the rest of the world, and that he couldn't work in a city anymore. Not isolation, but solitude, there was an important difference, she said. I took close note of everything she said, because as far as I was concerned Hemingway was speaking to us through her.

It was a beautiful early September afternoon, which passed far too quickly, all of us talking unselfconsciously about ourselves; she was Hem's (that's what she called him) fourth wife, they'd met in Paris after it was liberated from the Germans in 1944, where she was a reporter. Marie said she couldn't imagine being there so soon after the occupation, with the war still going on, and Mary said she was there and still couldn't imagine it, and that as bizarre as it all was, it was also terribly exciting and meeting Hemingway seemed at the time to make perfect sense; he felt as if he were born to be there, among the ruins of war and the excitement of liberation. What I remember most keenly is the fact that we all seemed to feel at home with one another, and that someone so strong-willed could also be so open-minded and warmly disposed. No one was trying to impress anyone else and that made it all the sweeter and then it was getting late in the afternoon and I said we should probably think about heading out soon, which is when she invited us to stay for dinner, saying two of Hemingway's granddaughters, whose names she didn't mention, would also be there. I guessed that it might be Mariel and Margaux because I'd read about them, and, excited at the prospect of meeting them, we both readily accepted. Which is when, moved by her gracious warmth, I asked if she would like my copy of *The Sun Also Rises*, it seemed only right that she, of all people, should own a first edition. She looked at me for a long time and, after gracefully declining what she called my very generous offer, asked me if I would like to see her late husband's study.

I said yes, of course, I would love to see it, having seen photos of his studies in Key West and his house outside Havana. And we were halfway up the stairs to the second floor when she stopped and, suddenly looking worried, asked Marie if she was a journalist writing about this visit. She never allowed journalists up there, or any photos to be taken. Marie looked stunned, as I must've, too. No, we both said. I then added that Marie carried her camera everywhere but would gladly leave it behind if she liked. Mary then said that she seldom showed anyone his study, especially complete strangers, and wasn't exactly sure why she was doing it now, but that I should take her wanting me to see it as a compliment. Her admission only made me want to see his study all the more, of course, and then we were there, standing inside Hemingway's study, as impossible as it was for me to believe.

It was a glorious room, with all his many books and one of his famous old Royal Quiet De Luxe typewriters, which he kept on top of a bookshelf, but he also wrote in longhand at his desk, she said, and then we all stood at the desk looking out the big picture window at the spectacular view of fields and distant mountains. I said I couldn't imagine writing anything with that majestic beauty surrounding me, and, her mood bright again, she said he preferred to write standing up and wouldn't even know where he was when he was writing. It was all just stunning, and I was speechless when, nodding at the desk, she said in a matter-of-fact voice that she could never quite understand, given how much he loved all this, why he had done it here of all places. I was so taken with the room and view and sense that I was actually meeting him, I asked what she meant—had done what?

I thought you understood, she said, this is where he killed himself.

Stunned and embarrassed, I said nothing.

Marie, sensing my alarm, took my hand. Feeling a little faint suddenly, I stood back against a bookcase, and sighed, deeply. Looking a little alarmed herself, Mary Hemingway asked if I was all right. I could barely hear her, or anything, and all I suddenly wanted was to get out of the room and house and back on the road. It was all a blur now and I didn't want to do or say anything stupid, and seeing how stricken Marie looked, I heard myself trying to explain that I suddenly wasn't feeling well and, much as I would like to stay for dinner, we wouldn't be able to. Though it was apparent that she didn't, she said she understood, and couldn't have been more gracious. And then we were all outside walking to my car and we all said goodbye and I promised to write and then, suddenly, I was driving down the hill, negotiating the sharp turns, feeling my heart through my shirt and jacket. It seemed only a few moments later, while we were passing a field of lush goldenrod, that I felt sleepy and couldn't keep my eyes open and stopped the car. Marie looked and sounded alarmed as I got out of the car and went into the field to lie down, saying I just needed to rest a few minutes by myself. The next thing I knew Marie was shaking me awake, saying that I'd slept for over four hours, and so deeply she couldn't wake me.

It was a long time before I could even think about what had happened to me there. Even now, all these many years later, I don't truly understand the connections I must've made between Hemingway's and my father's deaths, or the byzantine way in which I still feel complicit in my father's; I knew only that I was overwhelmed in a way I'd never been before or after, and that however different these two men were, seeing the place where Hemingway killed himself made me experience the degree to which I'd so confused his death with my father's. The manner in which I'd so completely absorbed into my being the loss they each represented.

Mary and I had exchanged addresses and wrote each other for a few years afterward; I would let her know where I was living and she would write short notes, commenting on her feelings about the places I would choose to live. Neither of us ever mentioned what had happened, though I always suspected that she somehow understood.

THE POET AND THE FICTION WRITER:
CONDUITS OF REVELATION

When I started writing, poetry was an esoteric school subject, the subject of eggheads, not tough street kids; poetry was for the sensitive types, to be scoffed at, at least as far as my father and all the men in my family and world were concerned, because anything that didn't make a living was an indulgence, inessential, extra. I felt compelled to be a fiction writer, like Hemingway, yet for a reason I didn't understand none of my fictional narrators were believable; they were all unrecognizable, self-referential extras without personality or affect, and the stories they felt compelled to tell were mostly autobiographical confessions and sketches intended only for one reader: myself. I doubt I ever stopped to even question whether a reader would find anything I was writing the least bit interesting. Perhaps because I equated fiction with success and poetry with being an extra, I felt freer, less anxious and visible, writing poetry. But the more successful my poetry became, the more I desired to write only fiction; editors who published my poetry were placed in the unenviable position of having to subsequently reject my fiction, while friends learned to be cautious when complimenting my poetry, knowing I could take it as an insult to my fiction. My every attempt to write became a permanent tug-of-war between visibility and obscurity, between the extra that wanted to be a star and the stranger who wanted to remain an extra: a perch so dubious and nondescript only a shitbird could find a home there.

For no reason I understood at the time I saw fiction writing as a shield against all my past bad luck, even though it seemed to bring me nothing but more bad luck. I went to grad school at Iowa to study fiction but switched to poetry for reasons I only partially understood; poetry seemed to offer me the kind of succor and refuge that others found in religion, a sanctuary or peaceable pause in which I could examine and escape all my failures in romance and in making a living. (I got by with odd jobs like driving a cab in college and grad school and between teaching jobs, the same thing my father did in his twenties, when he and three of his four brothers started a cab company in Fort Wayne, Indiana, that did well for a time, until he mismanaged it to the point where his brothers forced him out.) I thought I went to poetry for comfort and to understand my constant sense of dismay, but when I began publishing in visible places like the *New Yorker* and the *Partisan Review* in my late twenties, the fiction writer in me began resenting not only this success but the very idea of my wanting to be a poet. What I couldn't understand for some time was that poetry, and not fiction, was what offered me the reckless, lopsided unpredictability that I and my ego sought; that, yes, there were comforts to be found there, but the comforts of the abyss; it wasn't the haven that I believed I wanted.

Nevertheless, after my first book of poetry, *Like Wings*, was nominated for a National Book Award and won an American Academy of Arts and Letters award in 1979, I decided to take a break from poetry and write fiction full-time, a break that lasted more than six years. Most of this time was spent writing another autobiographical novel about an "I" who worked in the basement of a welfare building in San Francisco in 1968 while evading the Vietnam War

(the very material I later turned into my novel in verse, *The Wherewithal*, that was published in 2014; and yet another failed novel
about my family I later turned into a narrative book-length poem,
Living in the Past, published in 2002). My use of autobiographical
"I"s and not a persona to narrate these books prevented me from
stepping back far enough from my material to create the authorial
distance needed to imagine a story or plot; and without a clearly
perceived story to tell, my fictional characters were merely autobiographical ciphers and illustrations that essentially played the same
roles in the novel that they played in my life: symbols of concepts
and emotions I'd yet to explore. After the novel was rejected several
times by many publishers, I again turned to poetry, and when my
second book of poems, *Deep Within the Ravine*, won the Lamont
Prize, given by the Academy of American Poets, in 1984, a prize
given to the best second poetry book of the year, I managed to convince myself that unless I stopped writing poetry completely, or at
least stopped writing about those things that seemed to bring me
the most success, like my failed relationships and family history, I
would never find love or have a family of my own. The dark logic
my shitbird uses owns no sense of irony, apparently, because the
novel I then felt compelled to pursue for much of the next twelve
years was inspired by Henry Roth's *Call It Sleep* and dealt not only
with my mother and father but also the history of my misery in
romantic relationships.

The allure of such logic can be irresistible. I not only stopped
writing poetry for fifteen years but ended all my friendships with
poets, who comprised just about all my friendships (only Robert
Pinsky refused to acknowledge my never answering his letters or
invitations to submit my work, continuing to reach out as though
my silence were only a passing eccentricity, an act of friendship
he later attributed to mere obliviousness on his part). To be thor-

ough about my rejection of the poet in me, I also canceled all my subscriptions to poetry journals and stopped going to events having any relationship to poetry, which of course limited my ability to meet the kind of woman I believed I wanted to meet, the kind who would appreciate the poet in me. And since much of my identity was tied up with the world of poetry, I was in effect canceling out the only identity that nourished me, while failing to create a new one. Too jealous of the few fiction writers I knew to form any friendships, my relationships with my own sense of loss, abysmal failure, and loneliness seemed to be the only ones I was able to tolerate. In effect, I had recreated not only my father's world of failure but the one my friend Ralph lived in most of his brief life, the world of the extra and the exile, who lives essentially only in a world of dreams.

Yet the poet in me seemed to understand that despite whatever illusion I insisted on maintaining in my fiction—that my father was a larger-than-life character to be celebrated for his immigrant love of invention and his courage in the face of endless defeat—this period of abandonment of poetry (it was eighteen years between my poetry books *Deep Within the Ravine* and *The Holy Worm of Praise*) also served as a time of hibernation, and rejuvenation. It didn't seem to matter that I wasn't conscious of any of this. I would recognize subjects for poetry and sometimes even be nostalgic about ideas I wouldn't let myself write about, thereby acknowledging a desire I couldn't bring myself to appease. Many writers fear that in sharing their most intimate feelings something vital may be lost, that their most provocative and powerful beliefs should be kept private, if not secret. For me these secret feelings involved my father's failures and the shame I felt in having failed to save him, which I would allow myself to deal with successfully only in my poetry. It wasn't the fact that my poetry was successful that I so resented, but that it allowed me to connect with what I found most shameful in my life, and with authority and conviction.

Though my fiction did achieve some success early on—a novel I began when I was eighteen, *Amen, the Redeemers*, won me recognition and financial aid at the University of Louisville, while a later version helped pay my way through San Francisco State College, and stories fashioned from it won me acceptance into Iowa's graduate writing program, all perhaps due to the dramatic subject matter and scope of the project—I continued to write shapeless, emotionally disconnected novels and stories about this same subject for most of my twenties, my thirties, and well into my forties. I simply didn't know and probably didn't want to admit the truth—that my father was in fact and imagination a failure and, as far as I was concerned, a suicide. The anger I felt toward him for leaving my mother and me destitute wasn't something I could acknowledge in my writing until I was in my early sixties, when I turned to poetry to write my most successful poetry book, *Failure*, about this very subject.

Yet another irony is the fact that the story I was struggling to tell in both my poetry and fiction was a simple, straightforward one. When I was a sophomore in high school my father's vending business began to do well enough for us to move into a small two-bedroom basement apartment in the suburbs just across the city line. My mother, arguing that I needed to go to a better high school in order to get into a good college, had finally gotten what she always wanted, a place of her own. We lived there for two fateful years during which my father managed once again to duplicate the very formula behind all of his other failures: instead of selling his business to a larger vending company when it became interested, which would've afforded him the money and time to take it easy for the first time in his life, he decided to build the business up to increase its selling price, thus incurring debt for new vending machines, which eventually led to the stress and bankruptcy that killed him. But for two brief years we lived in our own home and my mother was the happiest I ever saw her. I'll never forget how proud and happy she looked when we first walked into our newly furnished, brand-new apartment. We ate in our own small kitchen and watched TV with the lights on. It was also a time in which I began to thrive in my new high school as an artist and writer both, winning recognition for my cartoons, stories, and, yes, poems, which also eventually won me acceptance at the University of Louisville, a place sufficiently far away from my father and his endless pursuit of failure.

This new high school was a public school in a well-to-do suburb, where many of the ambitious and privileged kids went on to first-rate colleges, and where, at first, I found it hard making any friends. I was an inner-city kid who wore velvet pants like some of my Black friends and loud colorful shirts like some of my Italian friends and danced in the exaggerated, go-for-broke unrhythmic style of my Eastern European friends, many of whom were academically and athletically uninspired. To say I stood out in this new, entitled environment would be an understatement. I quickly saw how useless my skill at fighting was here when a few of these new kids went out of their way to make fun of me; the one kid I asked outside for laughing at me in the lunchroom after he and his friends left the table as soon as I arrived reported me to the principal, who called my mother to school. I also learned quickly to keep a low profile and, well, just disappear, at least for a while. It was the beginning of my junior year and the pressure placed on students in this school was obvious; everyone worked especially hard, wanting to get into a good college, the exact opposite of the environment at my city school, where few took AP classes and most just wanted to do well enough to graduate and get a decent job at Kodak or Xerox, which was just starting in 1962.

But things changed when, in the fourth week of a class in international relations that I especially enjoyed, I chose to present a brief talk on Madame Chiang Kai-shek, aka Soong Mei-ling, for no reason other than that it was my turn to give a ten-minute talk and I liked the way her name sounded. It was a large seminar class with many of the smartest and most ambitious kids in this new school and I had no idea why suddenly everything I was saying about her role in her husband's defeat by the Communists' Red Army and retreat to Taiwan was so hysterically funny. But suddenly the two male teachers, who stood at the far back of the room to better observe the entire room, were obviously unable to restrain themselves. The taller one couldn't stop coughing and the shorter one left the room to laugh loudly in the hall. And once I understood I was being appreciated, I added funny faces and rude asides entirely made up, relating the Madame's reasons for dressing the way she did (lavishly flowered patterns without a hint of fashion) to inconsequential details about why Chiang Kai-shek's strategy for defeating the Japanese somehow limited his every attempt to move forward ten meager feet, and why Mao found it necessary to kill so many sparrows during and after the Chinese Civil War. It was for me a true moment of triumph that also quickly led to change. Never before had I held so much valued attention at will or realized that I could be witty and was something of a storyteller, just like my father. This was the first time that I realized that being recklessly different—in other words, being a poet—was a quality that could win the acceptance and approval I so very much desired. The prettiest girl in our grade, a girl named Marsha, was sitting right before me, beaming, welcoming every single thing I thought to say. She went out of her way to walk out of the class with me afterward, velvet pants and all, and to later sit with me at lunch. She had a college boyfriend, but it made little difference; we became friends, which changed everyone else's opinion of me and, to some extent, my opinion of myself. I even managed to win the support of a few of the smartest boys there, who offered me support and friendship after my father began to lose everything.

Which began in the middle of my senior year when my father's doctor called me to his office to tell me that my father had suffered a stroke and could soon suffer an even more serious heart attack unless he immediately stopped working and got medical attention. He understood I was busy getting into college and was in no position to take on such a large responsibility, but my mother had also failed to convince my father to stop working and there was no one else they could turn to. I tried to explain that I was the last person in the world my father would listen to, that he barely recognized my existence. Yes, the doctor said, but the sad truth was I was my father's best last chance to live.

At first my father would just laugh and walk away when I told him what his doctor said, and when I persisted, as I thought it was my duty to do, he would get angry and tell me to mind my own business. But now he could no longer afford to hire help and my mother was pleading with me to help him, so I went along with him to all his locations after school each day and on weekends, even Sundays, which, given the resentment that already existed between us, was the last thing in the world either of us wanted. Our new relationship became in a sense similar to the one that would later exist between the poet and fiction writer in me; to some inextricable extent, we became interdependent, unable to either accept or entirely reject the other. My father's weakened state seemed to get worse almost daily and the more dependent he became on me the greater his resentment grew, all of which only made me want to get as far away from him as I could. Our nightly arguments over dinner, when we were both exhausted and exasperated, grew more openly fraught and belligerent, until one night our words became physical.

We were both so tired neither of us had bothered washing up before dinner and we sat at the small kitchen table without speaking, avoiding each other's eyes. My father, as usual, pretended I wasn't sitting there, and sat staring at his hands, waiting for my mother to finish making dinner. Neither of us had spoken during the three hours we'd driven around together, and I'd considered skipping dinner, but didn't want to give him the satisfaction of my going hungry on his account. And I was in a very bad mood; I'd found out early that day that I'd been rejected from the college I wanted most to go to, the highly thought-of department of journalism at Syracuse University. Even though I hadn't really expected to get in—my grades were middling at my city school and I had low SAT scores (I never tested well because of my dyslexia, and had a hard time listening to instruction)—it was disappointing and only made being with my father all the harder. I'd told my mother about the rejection and then overheard her telling him, and though I didn't expect him to be consoling, I resented the fact that he didn't bother mentioning it. He didn't get past the seventh grade and didn't seem to care if I even went to college.

It was a tiny kitchenette, barely big enough to cook and eat in, and we were both staring at the floor, as if it would tell us what to do next. The silence became insufferable, and I heard myself doing what I knew he hated most: using the authority his doctor gave me to remind him of his weakened position. He was too weak to walk from a factory parking lot into a building, I said, my voice rising, he couldn't climb stairs or stop wheezing and coughing, and he was only getting worse—where did he imagine it would all end?

He didn't do what I expected; he didn't start yelling about who would take over his business and pay all our bills if he went into the hospital, or remind me of all the things I didn't know how to do, like tell the difference between the keys to the candy machines and the ones to the coffee and ice-cream machines or know the names of any of the bosses at the big factories. He just sat there, staring at me, his lips moving, as if rehearsing what he'd say next. Which is when my mother started pleading with us to stop arguing. Please, please, she begged us.

Please, just stop it, please stop fighting! she cried.

Which is when he said the one thing he knew, we all knew, would hurt me most. He asked me why, if I was so smart and knew everything, did the only school I wanted to go to reject me.

I could think of nothing to say or do. I sat there without speaking, staring at him. He once choked a man in a pool hall for stealing candy out of one of his vending machines, lifted the man off his feet and choked him until he stopped struggling and dropped him to the floor, where he lay gasping for breath, while my father went around the room handing out free bags of peanuts and candy bars, making jokes and trying to be funny, as if it hadn't happened, and the man wasn't lying dead still on the floor behind him, too frightened or hurt to move. The man was bigger, and probably stronger, but that didn't stop my father. Nothing seemed to stop him. I watched with horror, and curiosity as to what all the other men in the room would do. He had friends there certainly, and my father was supposedly there to serve them. But they did nothing, just watched with amazement, and then silently accepted his gifts, as though they had done something to earn them.

But now my father was the one who looked scared. I was much stronger than he, and he knew it. And he was losing everything, and we all knew it. And then I heard myself quietly telling him he didn't have to worry about which college I got into, if he kept working the way he was now he'd probably die soon, and we'd be penniless, and I probably wouldn't even go to college.

He got to his feet and walked across the tiny living room to my bedroom, the one place he knew he couldn't go. That was mine.

Yelling at him to stay out of my room, I got up and went after him, ignoring my mother, who was pleading with me to leave him alone.

He was tearing a sheet off my easel in the corner of the room near the windows. The sheet covered a portrait of him I was painting as a gift for his sixtieth birthday in three weeks. It was a portrait of him as a young man, taken from a photo of him and three of his four younger brothers, all smiling the same swaggering smile that dared the world to just try and get in their way. It was a smile that seemed to believe that they were starting from so far down that only contempt and defiance stood between them and extinction. But the emptiness behind this expression was obvious, too. The emptiness and the desperation.

It was a look very distant from the one he wore now, which was all desperation. I was about to try to explain this was a gift for his birthday that I'd been working on for weeks now, when he dropped the sheet and, without even glancing at the painting, began smashing the easel against the floor and wall. Mother was screaming at him to stop before he had another heart attack. And that's when, without thinking or even hesitating to consider the consequences, I went over and lifted him off the floor and yanked the easel out of his hands and then dropped him, the way he'd dropped the man in the pool hall, like an empty sack of clothes. Except he didn't fall to the floor like that man did, he went stumbling backward, arms flailing, until he collapsed against the wall and went sliding down to the floor, where he sat looking wildly up at me, panting.

It all happened so quickly all I could do was stand there and watch my mother trying to lift him to his feet, yelling at me now to help her. Whatever it was that I'd done wasn't something I could take back. And I wanted to help her, but I couldn't move, I just stood there, looking at the still wet canvas on the floor, at the splintered easel in my hand.

Then I ran over to him and tried to lift him, saying how sorry I was, that I never meant to hurt him, and that's when he said something I knew even then I'd never forget.

He said, Leave me alone, just leave me alone.

These were his last words to me. He died of a heart attack two months later. I went on helping him for weeks until he couldn't get out of bed one morning, but we didn't speak. I don't think he ever even looked at me again. He couldn't lift anything, and I did all the real work. I borrowed money from Jake and others to pay for his funeral and the $800 I took out of his vending machines kept us going until I managed to graduate from high school and we moved back into my grandma's house. To protect us from his debts, his lawyer placed his business in bankruptcy. Mother returned to the same filing-clerk job she'd worked at before she met my father and I found work over the summer in a roofing gang, replacing one of DuPont's roofs. Together, we saved enough money to help pay most of my first semester's tuition at the University of Louisville, where I went in the fall. Nobody, not my mother, my grandma, Jake, or I, seemed to feel any grief. We all seemed to be acting out parts in a script written by fate. When there were tears, they were tears of anger, or confusion, especially my mother's. The sorrow we felt wasn't for my father, it was for ourselves.

WHICH IS PERHAPS WHY MY first- and third-person fictional narrators were one-dimensional, autobiographical stick figures who saw their jobs as conveyors of factual information and little else, certainly not as storytellers who might engage their readers with anything resembling real emotion. Instead of recognizing the rich source of material this story contained and finding a narrator like Hemingway who might assert his rights as an objective surveyor over it, I instead felt compelled to praise and celebrate my father's great charms and accomplishments as an immigrant visionary, thus not only abnegating the pain I felt but forfeiting any right to the truth. The poet in me, in other words, was entirely muzzled and pushed aside. If I ever entertained any hope that writing about this material might lead to forgiveness, it was quickly repressed and buried. But in writing all this fiction I learned something about narrative structure and technique, which allowed me to eventually write my most successful book of poems, *Failure*, about that very subject. And in trying to help others find their stories I finally understood that the story I was trying to write wasn't about any of the things I thought it was. It wasn't about my father or mother, immigrant passion or forgiving the past, ambition or greed. It was about the self-imposed blindness and the lies I told myself in the belief that I was preserving some reservoir of privacy and self-respect; my real story was about the reasons I was protecting my father from myself and me from him, the ambiguities of self-delusion and the redemptive power of anger and shame.

Writers are conduits of revelation, not warehouses or depots of information, however entertaining or enlightening this information might be. Giving yourself permission to say what only you can say, finding the right style and form to express all this, requires an investigation into the cause and effect of old mistakes and wounds, into the realm of mixed feelings for what has been lost and left unresolved, all of which requires an act of self-forgiveness and deliverance. Discovering what a story or poem is really about, what it actually means under all the dross and confusion we create around everything that happens to us, has been perhaps the single hardest thing for me to do as a writer.

Only now, in fact, while writing this book, have I come to understand the extent to which I held myself responsible for my father's death in my fiction writing. The poetry persona narrators I used—Whitman, Bishop, Amichai, Babel, and, yes, Hemingway—all forced me to look at the story I was trying to tell as a story and not autobiography; the acute focus and concentration of the poetic voice forced me to distance myself not only from my material but from my shame.

OUR MOST CURIOUS ARTIFACT

Our most curious and personal artifact is something that doesn't own a skin color, religion, gender, or sexual orientation, something whose job it is to make us believe that regardless of how fragile, wounded, and subordinate we are to our fears and vulnerabilities, our existence is worth the enormous effort our survival demands. This something is the ego, our source of confidence and self-esteem. The ego mediates among all our competing roles and mysteries, renders the confusing and the unbearable tolerable, makes us believe that our story is worthy of being told, that in each line of every poem, each true sentence of every story, there is a commitment and responsibility to an aesthetic, the resonance of which provides us with our most valuable possessions: our contrition, benevolence, and vitality.

I could claim that it was my ego, or one of its surrogates, that brought me to New York City from Cambridge, Massachusetts, in 1976. I had a good teaching job in Boston, wonderful friends, and almost everything about my life there made sense, except perhaps one thing: I wanted something else, something more difficult, or even byzantine, to define; I wanted the kind of volatility that only a big city seemed to offer, to feel the way my writing made me feel, secular, unsafe, and selfishly resolute, to disrupt any sense of comfort I'd managed to accrue. I wanted to live according to the laws and customs of my most abstruse and perplexing commodity: my ego. And Philip Roth and, maybe especially, Norman Mailer provided quite lasting examples of just how one went about doing that.

I could also claim that in one way or other all or most of my teachers and mentors were stand-ins or replacements for my father, however much they were his exact opposite, or great improvements on his capacity to empathize and encourage. The writers I loved, especially Hemingway and Babel, were most certainly good models of how to succeed as a writer, though they never served as models of how to behave. They both died violently, Hemingway by his own hand, and Babel because his literary genius and reputation apparently threatened Stalin to the point where he had him executed. Babel in particular showed me a means of escaping the confinements of my past through ironic humor and visionary storytelling. By magically turning the horrors of war and shtetl life into hilarious tales of gangsters and ribald high jinks, I saw a way of escaping my own personal war and shtetl imprisonments. I was equally blessed with the writers and poets I met early on, in my twenties, like Philip Roth, Norman Mailer, George Oppen, Wright Morris, Joan Didion, Denise Levertov, Elizabeth Bishop, Philip Levine, and John Cheever, all of whom in some manner or form blessed me with their generous attention.

I met Philip Roth in Woodstock, New York, where Marie and I were spending the summer before my first teaching job, at Kalamazoo College, in 1971. I was twenty-six, had just finished my MFA at Iowa, and we were staying at an artists' retreat in Woodstock, where I was once again working on a novel and Marie found work in town at a photography shop. The retreat was designed for artists and I was their first writer, an experiment that for me was a miserable failure. Artists play music, loud music, and seem to visit one another's studios on a regular basis, and my little studio was in the midst of all this. I couldn't think, let alone write, and I spent my days walking around town, looking for a quiet coffee shop or park to read in, if not write. I was reading, coincidentally, Roth's novel about a hapless young woman, his only book with a female main character, *When She Was Good*, and one night, while I was in bed with a bad cold in the small room in town they gave us, Marie informed me that we had just been invited to Philip Roth's Fourth of July party at his house. I at first thought, her having seen his novel in my hands, that she was joking, and just shrugged and kept on reading. But she persisted, saying, yes, she had in fact met him in the post office in town, had mentioned that I was a writer and where we were staying and that I was miserable and couldn't write. I then asked if he'd tried to pick her up and she just smiled, which was answer enough. Though very intelligent and gifted as a photographer, she still dressed somewhat like a hippie, with long dresses and flowery blouses, her long blonde hair often tied up in two ponytails, and in fact her being picked up wasn't such a remote possibility; it was a constant source of strife between us and it was also how we met. I picked her up on a trolley in San Francisco, when we were both on our way to Berkeley for dates with other people—without a doubt, she was a beautiful woman, the kind who might catch Roth's eye.

This was two years after Roth published *Portnoy's Complaint*, and he was still going around in dark sunglasses and a big floppy hat, a disguise that was almost laughable, because his persona wasn't one that permitted successful camouflage for any real length of time; fame had helped mold and define it and it wasn't the kind that stayed hidden for very long. A prominent editor friend of mine, Kathryn Court, once described his persona to me as the kind movie stars own, that possessed an almost mythological aura shared by few other American writers. Perhaps because myth establishes its own boundaries and perspectives, the actual personalities inhabiting them often get pushed aside or lost, even to their owners. I may be flattering myself, but for whatever reason he seemed to feel comfortable enough around me to be completely himself, abstaining from both myth and performance of any kind. Perhaps it had something to do with the Jewish American immigrant world we both came from, a world in which humor and self-deprecation often enough served not only as an alternate reality but as a means of survival. Survivors of all kinds tend to recognize one another, especially if their means of surviving are somewhat similar. Laughter can be a salve against even one's own suspicious nature. Fame brings its own distortions, its own expectations and pretensions, and the fact that I've always failed at trying to pretend to be anyone more sophisticated or entitled may have allowed him to be a little more relaxed, if not trusting, around me. My genuine admiration for his talent, which eventually extended to the man himself, also probably didn't hurt matters any.

After I got to know him that summer, he would show me what he called "the crazy letters" from his mostly women admirers, some offering him proposals of marriage and nude photos. He was probably picking more up at the post office when he met Marie. In any case, we went to his party, where I also met Ivan Gold, the fine novelist and short-story writer, and many others of his New York friends, like Philip's lawyer friend Martin Garbus, who later let me use his garage to write in. Apparently, Woodstock was where many of the New York literati summered. But when Philip and I first met there was some awkwardness, if not tension. Marie had apparently led him to believe, or he had misunderstood her, that I was a published novelist on my way to teach at Iowa, when I had just graduated from there and, except for two short stories and a few poems, was essentially unpublished and on my way to my first teaching job in Michigan. When this came out in our first conversation, I went silent, thinking I'd disappointed him and had been invited under false pretenses. We barely spoke for most of the party and it wasn't until the end of the evening when he was saying goodbye to everyone that I took on some of the brashness of his own persona. He was coming over to say goodbye and before I knew what I was doing, I was telling him how impressed I was with him as a young writer who was just starting out and was no doubt flummoxed by all the obstacles and impediments thrown his way, and though he as yet lacked the confidence that comes from experience, if not success, his talent and desire were both obvious and impressive and I wanted to offer him every encouragement.

It was quite a mouthful, and I was exhausted by the time it all spewed out of me, exhausted and terrified. What in the world did I think I was doing! I'd just planned to thank him for inviting us and then slip back into my anonymity, where I was somewhat comfortable. Thank you, Mr. Roth, and goodbye. But now, everyone was staring at me, as if wondering perhaps whether this was an attempt at wit or a plea for help. Indeed, I had no idea where this role-reversing soliloquy had come from, or why, but my ego, seeing that I was about to lose a wonderful opportunity to meet an idol, found a more confident and less reverent and fearful persona to speak up for me.

Roth himself just stood there, with the smallest smile on his face, as if analyzing what he'd just heard; it was clear, however, that he was amused, if not intrigued. And then he started laughing, and everyone around us did, too, as if they'd all been waiting for permission. Everyone but me, that is, I was too stunned to speak, let alone laugh. What persona exactly had performed this aria—the fearless street kid, Hemingway the soldier and boxer, Babel riding off to the Polish front with his people's sworn enemies, the Cossacks? Or was it simply that the poet in me, seeing the fiction writer paralyzed with self-doubt, took over, using his fear of failure as motivation and intuition as a guide. It was then, too, that Marie, seeing that I needed a follow-up line or two, poked me in the back, and whispered, "It's your turn, again."

So, I said, "I think we should get together soon and straighten all this out."

Marie was glowing even before the other Philip invited us to dinner later that week and then went out of his way to find a more suitable place for me to write, in Martin Garbus's garage, which was quiet and perfect. He also sponsored me to Yaddo the following summer, where I could work in peace and quiet. We met for coffee and took walks, and I enjoyed getting together with some of his other friends, such as Ivan Gold, whom Philip also liked but once referred to as a frightened bear living with a frightened mouse, which made me wonder how he might one day characterize me, if he cared to highlight any of my flaws. But we stayed in touch after the summer ended and when I was at Kalamazoo College and wrote him that Marie and I had parted, he wrote back saying that he thought it was for the good, that however lovely and charming she was, she reminded him of his ex-wife, on whom he'd based the character Maureen Tarnopol, in his novel *My Life as a Man*. I had in fact tried to read that novel, without actually finishing it. It was an autobiographical novel about a highly manipulative woman who essentially tricks her husband, Peter, into an awful marriage, and who later dies in a car accident. Though I appreciated the good intention, I didn't know how to take this advice. Yes, Marie and I were a terrible match, and though I understood he meant well and was trying to help me in yet another way, I couldn't help wondering what she might've said or done that gave him that impression. Since she barely opened her mouth when we were all together, had they met separately? Her unfaithfulness was a constant source of dismay, but I hadn't mentioned it to him, though he may have inferred as much from just being around us. Roth was living at the time of our visit in Woodstock with a rather beautiful young woman, who was studying, if I remember correctly, philosophy at Columbia University, someone very much unlike his Maureen Tarnopol character, or even Marie, for that matter. It was probably obvious to everyone but me that we were highly mismatched; indeed, a number of my other friends had offered me similar advice. In some way or manner, I must've seen my own pain and confusion in people like Marie and Ralph Dickey, whose desperation and self-loathing somehow served as a kind of reflection of my own attraction to catastrophe; however tenuously, Marie and I were inexplicably keeping each other afloat, serving as a kind of life preserver or symbol of what in each of us was most worth salvaging. In any case, we managed to stay together for two more years after I met Philip, and I always wondered if he hadn't in some way seen in me something of his own shitbird, his own addiction to despair.

He told me that *Portnoy's Complaint* started out as a series of skits he wrote to entertain his Jewish friends in New York, and that they brought such a wild response he eventually wasn't allowed to show up without one. These skits were based on his life as a descendant of Russian Jewish immigrants in the Weequahic neighborhood of Newark, New Jersey, mixing in adolescent stories with his sexual adventures as a young man in New York City. Using crude Borscht Belt humor to tell the story of a brilliantly narcissistic and sexually addicted persona, he framed the narrative as a patient telling his story of woe to an analyst, which was based on another novel of Jewish self-flagellation, Italo Svevo's *Confessions of Zeno*. Published in 1923, Svevo's book was also one of my own favorite novels, a story that on its surface takes the form of a diary, in which a good deal of the sexual braggadocio is made hilarious by the merciless self-inquisition of the first-person persona, whose desire to confess everything to his analyst, and therefore himself, heightens the art of the kvetch to the level of self-heresy-and-sabotage. Though some critics found Roth's book an odyssey of Jewish self-loathing, a charge he understandably found painful, I found it a remarkable work of self-examination and comic genius. Nothing was off-limits here, nothing too sacrosanct to be made fun of—which made me wonder how I fit into all this. Was the manic quality of my relationship with Marie just another episode in the ongoing absurd theater of his own story? Was his attraction to me in some way similar to my attraction to Ralph—in warning me off Marie was he trying to save me from myself?

When I showed him a few of my published stories, he said they didn't go far enough with their subject matter, and though I didn't really understand what he meant, I decided, wisely I think, not to pursue showing him more fiction. And when I sent him a manuscript of poems, his only comment was that he didn't know enough about poetry to say anything helpful, which, interestingly enough, insulted only the fiction writer in me; the poet understood completely and was somewhat relieved. If I were going to burden him with requests for help, it would obviously have to be his idea, not mine. When, while living in Cambridge, I applied for a teaching fellowship at Harvard and asked him for a recommendation, he refused, saying he didn't know enough about my teaching to know what to say and didn't want to fake it. Faking it wasn't a problem for Norman Mailer, but I didn't get the fellowship and always wondered what Philip thought, if anything, about my winning the Pulitzer Prize for a book of poems about the kind of father he himself would've recognized only too well, and who would've fit snugly into his own cast of Jewish rogues and conniving outlaws.

I went to Yaddo the following summer, where all the other resident artists and writers seemed to know who'd sponsored me (I never learned how, and I avoided mentioning it, not wanting to be seen as a disciple of any kind), which gave me a small claim to temporary and unwanted fame. I later wrote him saying how very different it was from the artist retreat in Woodstock, and how grateful I was. We didn't get together again until many years later in New York, when Philip was married to Claire Bloom and teaching at the City College of New York. After learning from a mutual friend, Ted Solotaroff, that I was living there and directing the NYU graduate writing program, he called to ask whether he should keep his present health insurance or use the insurance the college was giving him. He wasn't used to teaching in a more formal context and thought since I was, I should know such things. I liked the idea that I was no longer the kid in Woodstock in his eyes, and therefore could be of use, and I advised him that since money wasn't the issue and he was used to his present policy he should keep it, just in case the teaching didn't work out. A year or two later, it didn't, apparently. The fact that it was understood that I'd established myself in the city, which wasn't exactly the easiest thing to do, and that he wasn't being asked to sponsor me anywhere or find me a place to write certainly made me a little more comfortable around him.

And then my friend the great Israeli poet Yehuda Amichai did what Marie had done more than a decade before, he brought us together again. Philip, who was greatly interested in Israeli politics and literature, very much admired Yehuda, who was in every sense Israel's national poet, a title less formal than it was honorific and all-inclusive. My friendship with Yehuda was also based on humor, if not irony, and to some extent, prophecy, mostly Yehuda's. He'd studied the Bible at Hebrew University and, being familiar with the Old Testament Prophets, liked to predict what many of my actions would amount to, especially those concerning the women I was seeing. Yehuda, who believed any form of self-employment for writers was a terrible idea, what he referred to as "freelancing," which he saw as a kind of slow suicide, never stopped trying to talk me out of leaving NYU in 1987 to start my own school. "See, there's your school in a few months, boychick," he once said, pointing to a boarded-up restaurant we'd eaten in a few weeks before and were now passing. When I told him I was going to buy and fix up an old wreck of a house in East Hampton after a recession in 1990, he feared it was too far away from New York to be of any use, I would never meet a woman out there, and since New York was the place for Jews, especially Jewish writers, the good side of my life was over and done with. Yehuda, whose family had escaped Nazi Germany in 1937, when he was thirteen, and had fought in four wars in Israel, certainly knew something about the true nature of the abyss, not to mention the good and bad sides of one's existence.

I'd helped in bringing Yehuda to teach in the NYU writing department when Philip, who'd met him a number of times in Israel, invited him to dinner at a Cuban restaurant in the Village, and Yehuda, thinking it would be more fun if I were around, invited me. Maybe Yehuda felt more comfortable around Philip when I was around, I can't say why for sure, but to some extent we all became not only more ourselves while together but, if possible, more Jewish. And being Jewish was what we all perhaps liked and knew best about ourselves. In any case, on this particular night anything any one of us said got an uproarious response.

The Cuban restaurant, only a few blocks away from where I lived on Charles Street, was a favorite of Philip's and when I repeated what Philip had once said to me about English Jews, that they weren't real Jews but pretend Jews, Yehuda said he himself didn't think anything at all about them, in fact, he did his best not to think of them at all, which, for whatever reason, struck us all as being the funniest thing we'd ever heard. Though I didn't know anything about them, I said that perhaps humor, because it probably wasn't translatable, never got translated into their brand of English. Philip liked this idea enough to add that English Jews could only be funny sitting down and everyone knew Jews had to stand up to be funny. It was also their British accent that got in the way, except for Philip Larkin, I said, maybe irony didn't work with such a pronounced accent. Irony, Yehuda added, was very expensive, especially when it was weighed in pounds. It was too heavy to carry around and you couldn't put it down because someone would steal it. We all found what everyone said, including ourselves, so hilarious we couldn't stop. Everyone else in the restaurant seemed to be enjoying us, too, including the waiters. There wasn't a lot of eating going on, in any case. Then Philip asked Yehuda what he thought about Cuban Jews, and Yehuda said he always wanted to meet one, but they obviously kept to themselves, maybe because you couldn't speak Yiddish in Spanish. Philip then wondered if our dinner was cooked by one, because no one seemed to be eating. The fact that Philip had lived in London and that his wife was both English and Jewish, made him something of an authority on the subject, though no one was deferring to him. I ended the conversation with a completely unnecessary insight: that in America Jews had to become more Jewish, it was expected of us, or at least that's how I always felt, especially because of writers like him, Saul Bellow, and Bernard Malamud, who'd made both American and Jewish literature more Jewish by default. I'm not sure I knew what I meant by this, but Philip certainly liked hearing it, as he also enjoyed experiencing the warmth of my friendship with Yehuda.

We got together a number of times after that, once for a Christmas Eve dinner—Jews love to make elaborate plans at Christmas, perhaps not to feel so left out—at the St. Regis Hotel off Central Park, Philip's idea, neither Yehuda nor I could afford such luxury, where Philip, in an especially lively and inventive mood, entertained us with rather lavish imitations of various literary figures, including his friend the gifted editor and writer Ted Solotaroff, whose opinions of his fellow writers and clients could be something less than adulatory. Ted could also be solemn to the point of appearing somewhat depressed, which fit perfectly into Philip's genius for zeroing in on the peccadilloes and often embarrassing characteristics of people's personalities and then enlarging them to comic proportion. On this one night, Yehuda and I not only enjoyed ourselves tremendously but then relived every moment of the evening on our walk home from Central Park West to the Village, some thirty blocks on a cold night that neither of us noticed.

The Jewish instinct for cornball zany humor often serves as insulation against the deprivations of diasporic despair, a kind of irreverent insulation that arose instantaneously when we got together, as if the traditions and paths of our various diasporas, Philip and I from mostly Polish and Russian descent, Yehuda from Germanic, would conflate into one vast conspiratorial theater of absurd complaint and self-mockery. And to the extent that this was true, it was impossible not to wonder why one couldn't maintain such self-regard and merriment when alone, but the need for a social context played no small part in Philip's genius for his often-comic illuminations of the absurd sexual and socioeconomic dysfunctions of his time. In his ever-evolving Nathan Zuckerman novels (*The Ghost Writer*, *The Anatomy Lesson*, *American Pastoral*, and *The Human Stain*, to name only a few), he found a persona narrator that allowed him to look at himself against the backdrop of his various ethical, political, and comic concerns while stepping in and out of his own past and present life with an ease and pleasure that often seemed both natural and extremely hard wrought. No other writer I can think of combined acts of outrageous mimicry with philosophical inquiry and, well, "crude" insight in so merciless a manner. Without doubt the persona he seemed to enjoy and inhabit most was the one he presented to himself, without reservation or caution. He knew who he was, he'd worked too hard to create himself not to enjoy his most successful work. This most personal and intimate mask gave him perhaps the greatest pleasure of all: the last laugh in a joke whose beginning was not only ancient but personal and endlessly confrontational. He was the comedian of the Torah, whether he knew it or not, though I think he did. His brilliant commentaries were mostly about what he thought about himself, and his time. The fact that we were all allowed to listen in is perhaps his most lasting gift.

SOMEBODY LOVES US ALL

It's the whole purpose of art, to the artist (not to the audience)—that rare feeling of control, illumination— life is all right, for the time being.

—ELIZABETH BISHOP,
IN A LETTER TO ROBERT LOWELL

It took me a long time to realize that the kind of reverence I felt toward Elizabeth Bishop's poetry was different from how I felt about the work of other poets I admired. It was a reverence that felt more intimate, and personal, and somewhat frightening, as if she were somehow writing to me alone, or attempting through her poetry to advise me on how to survive whatever degree of unhappiness and jeopardy I was suffering at the time. Even her remove from her subjects, so elegantly descriptive in "A Cold Spring," in which the "you" she addresses is the owner of "big and aimless hills," and "the light, against your white front door," is as withheld and private as it is sumptuously lyrical and engaging: "And your shadowy pastures will be able to offer / these particular glowing tributes / every evening now throughout the summer."

Hers is a voice as rare as it is genuine, a passionate alchemy derived from endless lyrical experimentation and self-examination. If I were ever to be a real poet—one who apparently enjoyed thinking of himself as one—this was the kind of voice I would like to speak in, the kind I used to speak to myself in when I most needed verification and reassurance, the kind that seemed to come from so dark and precarious a place in herself. Orphaned first by her father's death when she was eight months old, and then by her mother being permanently institutionalized in a mental hospital when she was five, raised first by strict grandparents in Nova Scotia and her wealthier paternal grandparents for a short time, and then by an aunt and abusive uncle in Worcester, Massachusetts, where she was born, her book titles alone—*North and South*, *Questions of Travel*, and *Geography III*—outline a peripatetic childhood in which she was sent back and forth among family members, some of whom were abusive. No wonder, then, the question she poses in the last lines of her great poem "Questions of Travel": "Continent, city, country, society: / the choice is never wide and never free. / And here, or there . . . No. Should we have stayed at home, / wherever that may be?"

Though purely feminine in nature, and without all the posturing and masculine artifice, her persona seemed to view the world with the same elegant distance and strength as Hemingway's, a strength that seemed in every way as earned and designed. I was first introduced to her work in college, at San Francisco State, in a class on modern poetry, taught by the very self-possessed, intensely studied, and brilliant poet Jack Gilbert, that dealt with the Beats and worked its way up to the New York Poets, John Ashbery, and Frank O'Hara, and finally Theodore Roethke, Robert Lowell, and Bishop. We covered poems from her earlier books, *A Cold Spring* and *Questions of Travel*, discussing individual wonders such as "At the Fishhouses," with its eye for precise, detailed description; the great loving celebration of her idol and mentor in "Invitation to Miss Marianne Moore"; and the vibrant horror of visiting Ezra

Pound imprisoned in a mental institution in "Visits to St. Elizabeth," which so powerfully uses the English nursery rhyme "The House That Jack Built." My favorite, though (until the collection *Geography III* came out in 1976, with her ten great poems, among them "In the Waiting Room," "The Moose," "One Art," "The End of March," and "Five Flights Up"), was "Filling Station," narrated in the bittersweet voice of a child observing what must've been to the young Elizabeth a bewildering view of adulthood—"Oh, but it is dirty! / —this little filling station," a voice startled by its own delight, and that finds its all-encompassing affirmation in the last stanza:

> Somebody embroidered the doily.
> Somebody waters the plant,
> or oils it, maybe. Somebody
> arranges the rows of cans
> so that they softly say:
> ESSO—so—so—so
> to high-strung automobiles.
> Somebody loves us all.

Yes, somebody loves us all—the poet's need to feel precious to someone, anyone, even a complete stranger in a gas station, reveals so enormous an affirmation in so plain and simple a manner it comes as a complete surprise. It was the kind of vulnerability revealed in James Wright's "Lying in a Hammock at William Duffy's Farm in Pine Island, Minnesota," which ends with an equally unforgettable tagline: "I have wasted my life." What precedes this line in Wright's poem is as innocently undramatic and unexpected as what precedes Bishop's: a description of lying in a hammock watching a butterfly sleeping on a black tree trunk, hearing cowbells ringing in the distance, when the narrator leans back to watch a chicken hawk fly past, looking for home, he imagines. This is when he so casually gives us this last, devastating line: "I have wasted my life." I cannot count the times I witnessed this technique imitated in college and graduate school by poets who had no idea whatsoever why Wright's line evoked so profound an emotional response. Editors of good poetry journals complained of dreading seeing so many poems about everything from birthday parties to elegies for pet rabbits ending haphazardly with such lines pasted onto the end, without any apparent idea by the poets that emotional resonance of this kind had to be earned by what came before, often at great emotional expense. But Bishop's was the first American poem I read that so exemplified this kind of manifest suffering with such subtlety and sense of inevitability.

The profound sense of emotional deprivation I felt in her poems seemed unlike anything I'd read before, the almost casual urgency of the speaker, a persona personality so torn between prudence and self-possession I felt as if I needed to ask permission before assuming, for instance, that the Friday who "died of measles / seventeen years ago come March" in her poem "Crusoe in England" is, has to be, her partner of seventeen years, Lota de Macedo Soares, who committed suicide after their relationship ended painfully. Yes, Crusoe is looking back and ruminating on a quickly fading past, a Crusoe who tells us in an almost offhanded way, "Just when I thought I couldn't stand it / another minute longer, Friday came." A Friday whom Crusoe wishes were a woman so they could propagate his own kind, believing Friday wished the same thing. This is quite a statement, spoken behind the guise of a persona so unassuming and matter-of-fact it feels rude and intrusive to question his/her meaning. Is there a literal subtext here; did Bishop ever imagine that her happy relationship with her nice Friday (in real life, the wildly flamboyant and outspoken Soares, Bishop's opposite in every way) might lead to some further sense of permanence, did she ever wish for children? Her Crusoe persona also allows her to deal with her exile in Brazil for so many years, and the isolation and loneliness that came before and after her happiness. It didn't seem to matter that I understood nothing of the underlying autobiographical intimations of her poems, what mattered was that I was hearing echoes of my own loneliness and desires to settle down and have a family being addressed on a level I found both comforting and terrifying. And not only my own sense of exile and unhappiness, but my friend Ralph Dickey's suffering too.

Ralph's musical Monk/Coltrane persona also dealt with his intense feelings of being cast aside that plagued him throughout his brief life; he too sought a somebody who loves us all. The isolation he expressed in his poem "Leaving Eden," where "the cries of my bones / like the cries of animals / followed me out of my mother / into exile," isn't all that different from what Bishop's young girl is suffering in "In the Waiting Room," where, after hearing her aunt's cry of pain in her dentist's office, the poet/child brilliantly summarizes the emotional impact of her life thus far: "The waiting room was bright / and too hot. It was sliding / beneath a big black wave, / another, and another." The big black wave is her premonitions of womanhood perhaps, a future in which "the War was on." Though their styles differ vastly—Ralph wrote his lines when he was in his early twenties, a graduate student at Iowa, while Bishop wrote hers near the end of her life, in her mid-sixties—each knew well the effects of extreme deprivation, of the big black wave of abandonment and abuse, each struggled to survive an endless war of attrition through poetry and music. Bishop found the love she sought more often and for longer periods of time, though her form of slow suicide through drink and drugs was just as fatal finally; she died of a cerebral aneurysm at the age of sixty-eight, Ralph by his own hand when he was twenty-seven.

Though I understood none of this when I first read her poetry, the reverence I felt was in some mysterious and profound way intertwined with the distilled and intense vehemence of my own ambitions as a writer. Writing for me also was a means of survival, the infinite number of drafts of each poem a struggle for ultimate self-realization and self-forgiveness, the stark questioning of my every motive and intention a desire to justify my irresoluble sense of shame for feeling complicit in my father's death. In her beautifully reconstructed ocean world of Nova Scotia in "At the Fishhouses," where she wonders if tasting the cold dark seawater would be "like what we imagine knowledge to be: / dark, salt, clear, moving, utterly free, / drawn from the cold hard mouth / of the world," she seemed to be asking the most essential question of all, the very question her, my, and Ralph's shitbirds desired most to turn against us—does understanding why we suffer make the suffering worthwhile? Does knowledge bring redemption, allow in any way our becoming "utterly free . . . of the world"?

Her extraordinary poem "One Art" is perhaps the closest we'll come to an answer, or the intimation of one. I believe it was the last poem she saw published before her death, a villanelle in which her loss of Soares and what then appeared to be a final separation with her new and last love, Alice Methfessel, are exquisitely intertwined in the final quatrain: "—Even losing you (the joking voice, a gesture / I love) I shan't have lied. It's evident / the art of losing's not too hard to master / though it may look like (*Write* it!) like disaster." Does this suggest that though it may look like disaster, it isn't really? She had to know where her constant drug use and drinking were taking her, that it most certainly would lead to real disaster. For Ralph, exile was a permanent state, answered only by death. Bishop, I don't believe, ever stopped looking for the home that had been taken away from her, and for a Friday. Though she found contentment during the final years of her life in her relationship with Alice Methfessel, who was thirty-two years younger than she, and to whom she dedicated *Geography III* and left everything she owned in her will, the hard-earned taste of knowledge of which she so movingly wrote, the kind that in her case inspired lyrical genius, was, as far as I was concerned, not about literary ambition, or seeking the kind of veneration that art at the highest level provides, but knowing the kind of love that staves off actual disaster, or makes one relive it repeatedly throughout one's life.

I TOO HAVE LED A peripatetic life; after leaving home, I moved from Louisville to San Francisco; then Iowa City and Kalamazoo; then Taos, New Mexico; Sheffield, Vermont; then Provincetown and Cambridge, Massachusetts; then New York City, where I met my wife in a dog park in my late forties; and finally settled down in East Hampton to raise a family. It also took me a long time to find love, and a home. I can say with some confidence that the alchemy of a genuine poetic persona derives not only from ambition, hard work, and technical ingenuity, but a sense of personal insecurity so forbidding and painful it fosters endless self-examination. Then why, given so many opportunities to meet her in Cambridge, through friends and poetry readings and occasions, did I somehow manage so successfully to avoid doing so for the entire three years I lived there? Was I afraid that the actual person would in some manner impair the comfort I received from her poetry? Was I attempting to spare myself further disappointment? I wasn't afraid to meet so many male writers, or father figures—why was this so different? Did it have anything at all to do with what a female poet I knew in Cambridge once told me about what Bishop had said to her over lunch? I didn't think so, though it wasn't something I could easily overlook or dismiss.

They were friends, she said, often meeting to discuss everything from poetry to more personal matters, though never anything as personal as what Bishop brought up when she last saw her. Apropos of nothing they were discussing, Bishop suddenly told her that, because she was a wife and mother, relationships that demanded so much of a woman, and given how much time and attention a career in the arts also required, it wasn't likely she would become the kind of poet she so desired and was so capable of being. She was a few years older than me—I was twenty-eight and she, I thought, in her mid-thirties—and well thought of as a poet and writer. She had believed she knew Bishop well, well enough that she could only sit there, across the table from Bishop, staring at her. Had she said or done something to anger or upset Bishop in any way? she wondered. She understood there was much female artists of Bishop's generation had to overcome in patriarchal societies, and Bishop, after all, was the first female to teach poetry writing at Harvard on a full-time basis, and aware enough of her role as a major female poet to refuse to be included in anthologies of female poets on the basis that there weren't any of just men's poetry, that literature wasn't, as far as she was concerned, something that could be subdivided according to gender, race, or religion, it was simply literature. Bishop, most likely, my friend said, meant to be instructive, and, perhaps, even kind. But it was also an unwarranted thing to say to someone who looked up to her as a friend and mentor. She wasn't, after all, a young single woman just starting out, to whom such a statement could be construed as a warning, she already had a family she loved and valued, one that couldn't easily be tossed aside.

Though I understood that such an intimate revelation called for a reassuring and comforting response, one perhaps that offered a more objective perspective, hard as I tried, I could think of nothing adequate to say. I just stood there, nodding, wondering what may have inspired this comment—in Bishop's work, suffering usually led to knowledge, the kind of self-awareness that overcame envy, regret, or fear of the road not taken. Her work in so many ways was her life, and often it's hard, if not impossible, to translate into our lives what we come to in our work. In reading the letters between her and Robert Lowell many years later, I was taken by the degree of intimacy their friendship engendered, a love, certainly on Lowell's part, that was as sexual in nature as it was collegial and empathetic—was she once more regretting that Friday wasn't a woman and that the personal cost of perfection was at times too great? On some level, I realized that all of this just wasn't any of my business; that I wasn't really entitled to even wonder why she would say such a thing.

DURING MY FIRST YEAR IN Cambridge, I lived in a small studio apartment in a five-story apartment building that once had been a Harvard dormitory, where, as another tenant claimed, Teddy Roosevelt had lived as a freshman. I spent my mornings looking for a teaching job while driving a taxi at night and unloading computers from trucks in the afternoon. At night I would sometimes stand at my front window that looked out over Harvard Square and the campus to my right, with my hands folded behind my back, as I imagined Mr. Roosevelt had stood. Marie and I were now officially separated, and though I would occasionally see her on the street hurrying to work—she waitressed in a restaurant off the Square— we would each appear flummoxed and apologetic the few times we actually ran into each other, as if the finality of our separation had established itself without our consent. Previously, our sadness felt mutually ascribed to, attached like an affidavit of ownership; now it felt individual, separate, and therefore somewhat less hopeless. It was our new lives that seemed to be avoiding each other, not us; we somehow remained the same. Did any of us ever know who we were or where we were going or why? What I seemed to know was that I never wanted to be anyone else, I was too curious to discover how I would turn out, given the odds for and against me. I thought of another poem of Bishop's that I'd recently read in the *New Yorker*, "Five Flights Up," one that seemed to be addressing my own view of the world from my own five-flights-up perspective:

FIVE FLIGHTS UP

Still dark.
The unknown bird sits on his usual branch.
The little dog next door barks in his sleep
inquiringly, just once.
Perhaps in his sleep, too, the bird inquires
once or twice, quavering.
Questions—if that is what they are–
answered directly, simply,
by day itself.

Enormous morning, ponderous, meticulous;
gray light streaking each bare branch,
each single twig, along one side,
making another tree, of glassy veins . . .
The bird still sits there. Now he seems to yawn.

The little black dog runs in his yard.
His owner's voice arises, stern,
"You ought to be ashamed!"
What has he done?
He bounces cheerfully up and down;
he rushes in circles in the fallen leaves.

Obviously, he has no sense of shame.
He and the bird know everything is answered,
all taken care of,
no need to ask again.
—Yesterday brought to today so lightly!
(A yesterday I find almost impossible to lift.)

Yes, for her everything is answered, finally. The question is where and how she managed to find such faith and promise. Was there something beyond our knowing that was looking after us, capable of answering all our impossible questions? While standing at my window one early evening, I spotted who I at first thought was Marie walking unhurriedly down the street, but then I realized Marie never walked unhurriedly anywhere, especially if going to work, and never with a bounce or sense of purpose and resolve, she was always rushing everywhere, as if late for work, often enough feeling somewhat harassed. And when this woman vanished into one of the campus entrances, I wondered if this could've been Miss Bishop herself, on her way to her class, perhaps rehearsing in her mind something she would say about her essential art. I couldn't be absolutely certain it was her, viewed from my perspective in the growing dark, not with all the day's long colors blending into the heated blur of twilight, but Bishop would walk this way, I was convinced, with a slight bounce, and sense of purpose and resolve, as if each step were a line break, a casually deliberate caesura finding its own perfect cadence, that "ponderous, meticulous . . . gray light streaking each bare branch." Yes, it was she, or so I was inclined to believe, and perhaps in an oddly fateful way, we were finally meeting, or at least it pleased me to think so.

PENURIOUS ARROGANCE

I was always somehow aimed at New York and considered every place I lived in previously as a kind of way station. Or, as Norman Mailer put it to me, "It's the place for any writer of ambition, whether they can admit it or not." I pretended to know what he meant as I did with most things he told me, especially so when I had little idea what he was talking about. But, yes, I was ambitious—for what, exactly?—which he obviously liked about me. I stayed in his place in Brooklyn Heights (the top floor of a brownstone he once owned entirely and now only owned the top floor of, a matter of taxes, he said, he was always struggling to pay his taxes) while I was looking for an apartment in New York in 1976, when he also advised me to find a place in Brooklyn, that I didn't need to have "it all at my doorstep." But I'd always dreamed about living in Greenwich Village and that's where I ended up and still own a small place on Charles Street. Marie and I had broken up in Cambridge and I enjoyed being by myself in Norman's place, reading the massive manuscript of his novel *Ancient Evenings* that he was working on and just happened to leave out on the big table that divided his study from the living room, where I couldn't miss it. I was flattered that he cared enough about my opinion to want me to read it, but in all truth I found it hard going and not only because I was a slow reader; it was densely written and imagined, without much of a plot and though there was a good deal of Mailer's flair for description, graphic sexual intrigue, and vigorous reportage about an entirely imagined and far-removed world, I read just enough to be able to comment on it with a kind of diluted authority. When I wasn't in the city looking for an apartment I could afford, I spent my time working out on his gym equipment, which seemed to be everywhere, even in his tiny kitchen. Somehow every time I tried to write, his mother, who lived down the block, managed to appear. She enjoyed talking to me about all the famous people she'd met through her son, like Kissinger and Truman Capote, and she claimed I reminded her of Norman when he was my age, only I was even skinnier. I was just turning thirty years old, and entirely broke, which seemed to be one of the things he liked about me, given that I was gambling, as he saw it, everything on a lifestyle—I assumed he meant poetry, the only time I showed him some of my fiction he put his arm around me and said, "Señor, the good news is you're a poet, and the bad news is, well, you're a poet." Born of dubious risk and intimidations, maybe that was how we both saw a life in poetry. Though I could add, too, that my willingness to box with him and get hit in the face every time a woman passed by was no doubt another aspect of that risk-taking.

I first got to know Mailer at a party at his house in Provincetown, Massachusetts, where Marie and I were spending the winter between my teaching jobs. I was working on the same thankless novel about San Francisco and my welfare experience and was hanging out at an early incarnation of the Fine Arts Work Center there, which was at the time run by Mary Oliver, whose partner, Molly Malone Cook, a very good photographer, also served as Mailer's secretary. My landlord, Ciro Cozzi, owned a popular restaurant, Ciro & Sal's, that Norman frequented when in town and, thinking we should meet, Ciro introduced me to him one night at the bar. I was Ciro's idea of a starving writer and though I didn't find it out until I left town, he never cashed any of my rent checks, his idea, I imagine, of sponsoring the arts. I was living off what small savings I had left from teaching at Kalamazoo College, Marie and I once again were not getting along (she pretty much came and went with whomever she pleased), and I'd just heard from a friend in San Francisco that my friend Ralph Dickey had killed himself. I couldn't even begin to absorb the truth about his death and lived in a fog that promised never to lift. I hadn't yet received many details from our mutual friend, Michael Harper, who was Ralph's power of attorney and literary executor, and Marie, unable to deal with her own grief for Ralph—the three of us were inseparable in our last years in San Francisco—stayed as far from mine as she could, which only added to my remorse. If I looked half as bad as I felt, it's no wonder Ciro seemed desperate to lift my spirits and figured Norman Mailer was the perfect person to do it.

Mailer was drinking heavily at the time and I barely touched the stuff, and not only because I couldn't really afford it; I knew my ego could be fragile and easily mistake flattery for insult, and I tended to stay away from booze and drunks. But Mailer was famously brilliant and very funny and everyone at the bar was hanging on his every word. What most attracted me to him was his own unique kind of reckless unpredictability, an ego that seemed to take pride in placing what it deemed most outrageous about itself on public display. Even Roth's persona, which seemed pleasantly civilized and tame in comparison, couldn't compete for the kind of raw privilege and attention Mailer's demanded of the most casual respondent. In any case, Ciro introduced us, telling Mailer that when I first pulled up to his house right off Commercial Street, the main street in town, in my old wreck of an Opal station wagon, with everything I owned piled up in back, he thought I looked as broke as anyone he ever saw, knowing Mailer would somehow see this as a sign of my seriousness as a writer. And then Ciro abruptly left, and Mailer was again surrounded by a number of mostly drunken young men vying for his attention, not sycophants exactly, more a choir of revelers seeking a conductor for their loutish symphony. It seemed neither the time nor place to talk, but, yes, the grandiosity of Mailer's persona, which he seemed to wear like a suit of armor, made for a good distraction from my grief, and when I could think of nothing to say, he, perhaps sensing my self-consciousness, laughed and said, "Don't tell me, you're in town scouting the place for an *Esquire* article on nightlife among the cannibals." No, I said, I was doing one on the difference between being rich and famous and nervous and dirt poor. He sat back on his stool and gave me one of his rather famous and curious squints, as if he wasn't entirely sure he hadn't been insulted, and then said, "You don't look all that nervous." I said I was building up to it and he laughed again, and then ordered both of us another drink and said that he'd seen me around town looking "penuriously arrogant" and when I asked what "penurious" meant (I really wasn't sure, but that didn't seem to matter) he laughed loudly and then gave me his phone number and suggested we get together late some afternoon when he'd finished writing. Which we did whenever he was in town. Provincetown, he later explained, was where he came to do his best writing, especially in the fog-encrusted quiet of the winter.

Oddly enough, except for *The Naked and the Dead*, which I read in college, and some essays and his journalism, I'd never really read much of his work, perhaps because, knowing his great admiration for Hemingway—he once said in an interview that the emotion in each of Hemingway's books had the intensity of first novels, meaning, I imagined, that his wholehearted and genuine enthusiasm for what he was writing about was always on display—I expected that to some degree his work would only remind me of my own infatuation with Hemingway. But I then began reading *An American Dream* and was completely engrossed with the immediacy and casual formality of his first-person narrator, Stephen Rojack, whose direct address to the reader, with its uninterrupted attention and focus, struck me as being completely original. His obsession with violence—he kills his disturbed wife and finds himself, along with the reader, on a kind of Jack Kerouac road trip through the various precincts of hell—was no doubt an exploration of Mailer's own appetite for extreme, if not obscene, social and sexual obsession. I certainly didn't detect any real stylistic influences between him and Hemingway; unlike Hemingway's short declarative and lyrical sentences, Mailer's looped across the page like snakes obsessed with swallowing their own tails, and there was little to none of Hemingway's indirection and restraint. I began to wonder whether there was a connection here between Roth's attraction to the crude and Mailer's to the extreme, and if their egos sought inspiration only at the fringes of civilized behavior. I found Mailer's ability to imprison so extreme a personality in a noirish, somewhat lurid plot, using the perversity of Rojack's persona to experiment with his own tolerance, if not capacity, for violence, captivating and began reading his other novels, *The Deer Park* and *Armies of the Night*, enjoying how each narrator allowed him to focus on yet another aspect of his own personality, often using that aspect, like his obsessiveness, to drive the narrative along. There was never much plot or expected character development, it was all his own fascination with the peculiarities of his characters' egos, as if he were daring his reader to find their own obsessions any the less fascinating.

Not knowing until the last moment if we were moving there together, Marie and I moved to Cambridge later that spring. Because I really wanted to be in New York, and was feeling both hopeful and despondent, Cambridge, and Boston, seemed a reasonable place to find work and figure out what to do next. We found an apartment in the basement of a house in Somerville, almost within walking distance of Cambridge and about five miles from Boston across the Charles River, and Marie went about finding a job while I for the first few months drove a cab, unloaded computers from trucks, and then found a teaching job at what was then Newton College of the Sacred Heart, a Catholic girls' school, where I taught one class of creative writing and then found another teaching job at Tufts University, teaching basic English to freshmen. At one point, I had two teaching jobs at two different schools while driving a cab at night, the idea perhaps being to keep myself too exhausted to deal with the fact that Marie was now moving into her own place in Cambridge, a split that felt both necessary and permanent. But now I was losing both Ralph and Marie, two-thirds of the desperate triumvirate we'd composed in San Francisco for what then felt like an eternity but was closer to two years. Lonely and dejected, I focused on finding a full-time teaching job, which I got later that winter, at the University of Massachusetts at Boston, after going to an interview between taxi rides, my breathless demeanor somehow working in my favor, at least that's what my interviewer told me, a Philip Sidney scholar who said the fact that I seemed to be in between more urgent things lent me an air of stoic "insouciance" that made me more appealing than the other more focused applicants.

Norman would call when he came to town and though he understood Marie and I had been together nearly five years and that I was having a hard time adjusting to my new life alone, he never once mentioned her. I imagined it just didn't seem a big thing since he was now living with the jazz singer Carol Stevens, whom he would soon leave for his sixth wife, Norris Church. He also probably just assumed I knew what I was doing, even if I didn't. It was around this time that he began inviting me up to Stockbridge, where he lived with Carol and their daughter Maggie, and on my first trip there, Mary Oliver and Molly Cook arranged for me to drive two of Mailer's young sons, Michael and Stephen, from his previous and fourth marriage with Beverly Bentley, up to Stockbridge, where I'd no sooner gotten out of my car than Norman put boxing gloves on me and said, "Let's see what you have, hombre." Ominous words. Kids in my old neighborhood slugged at each other, with and without gloves—who could afford boxing gloves?—mostly flailing our arms about and shouting insults at each other while only occasionally landing a punch. But Norman wanted a sparring partner and that's what I became. He was a good teacher, patient and interested in what he saw as an art form, while I enjoyed using all my old street-game tricks, feinting and twirling to the side to avoid his mostly playful swings meant more as instruction than landing punches or making points. But when a woman was even in the vicinity of his backyard, where we sparred, he'd suddenly become someone else altogether, not exactly a Dr. Jekyll and Mr. Hyde transformation, because in his case the change didn't appear to be entirely voluntary or conscious. He must've assumed I could handle being hit in the body or face or he probably never would've put gloves on me in the first place, though mostly we danced about in a kind of pedagogical trance, gossiping about the inanities of various other contemporary fiction writers, while Norman showed off his rather sophisticated knowledge of the art of fisticuffs. But the first time his wife Carol stopped to say hello to me, and I turned my head to reply, I found myself lying flat on my back, having water splashed in my face. And there was Norman, on his knees next to me, pounding the earth with his gloved hand, cursing himself. I was too groggy to even attempt to comfort him, if that's what he wanted, though it soon became clear that his capacity for guilt was nearly as great as his appetite for just about everything else, especially women—he was married six times, and sired eight kids, adopting a ninth.

After boxing, we'd sometimes hike in the mountains not far behind his house and during one of these hikes we began getting restless and maybe a little bored with all the straight-up climbing and obligatory commenting on all the beautiful views. Yes, the view of the valley below, where we could see his house, was quite beautiful, but what was missing quickly became clear to both of us: any excitement. It was taken for granted when we got together that there should be some kind of excitement—it in fact seemed de rigueur to our getting together—and he was telling me about a nonfiction book he was working on at the time—a biography of Marilyn Monroe, I believe—and I was only half listening, not because it wasn't interesting, which it was, but because I was worried about moving to New York soon without a teaching job waiting for me. I was grateful to Norman for offering to let me stay in his Brooklyn Heights place while I looked for a place of my own, though I wasn't entirely comfortable with the idea of feeling indebted to him, or anyone. For one thing, he'd seen so little of my work that his faith in me seemed to be based entirely on his instincts and hunches, which to some extent made me feel less secure about my prospects; perhaps, too, I was worried about disappointing him. And I was about to say what I thought would be witty, or "cute," a word he liked, that I was planning to write a book based on *The Prisoner of Sex* called *The Prisoner of Poverty*, when we suddenly turned a corner of a rather steep path and found ourselves standing on a ledge that overlooked what seemed the entire vista of Stockbridge and the Berkshires beyond. This truly was a beautiful view of the world and we both stood there in quiet amazement, when he gave me a look I'd grown to know only too well: a look of competitive and anxious curiosity. It was the look he sometimes had when we boxed, of sheer extroverted self-absorption.

In an instant, without hesitating, we began running full-out toward the edge that overhung the valley below in an unannounced game of chicken that had only one rule: the first to stop before going over the edge lost. As a kid, I almost never lost a game of chicken, maybe because losing meant the kind of spectacular humiliation all us first-generation kids knew only too well: the shame of never being good enough, the kind of lifelong captivity that required constant renovations of the self. Norman was also first-generation—his father was born in South Africa, coming here by way of England, his mother the daughter of a rabbi—and many of his personas were designed to prove that he was no longer a nice Jewish boy from Brooklyn, which is perhaps why Hemingway's persona of masculine vainglory served us both so well.

And now we were both running all-out toward what looked like the edge of the world, our breath exploding, the same absurdly wild smile on both our faces in a contest that depended entirely on the concept that losing wasn't a possibility. But he was nearly twice my age and with a belly not made for sprinting, which is what we were doing now, sprinting toward the heavens on a gorgeous fall day, each lost somewhere in the fog of our own and each other's ego system, wanting not only to win but to beat and render the other a loser. And I was loving the idea that I was faster and didn't even pause to consider where my momentum was taking me, until, with one foot hanging suspended in mid-air over the edge and the realization of impending doom suddenly fogging my vision, Norman reached out and grabbed my shirt and yanked me back, both of us falling to the ground and then rolling over ourselves. Wildly panting and roaring with laughter, he yelled, "You crazy motherfucker, you were going over, you know that—you're a fucking maniac!"

However infantile and stupid our actions, it no longer seemed to matter who won or lost, we now both owned a story that we could turn, at least in our own minds, into myth. Norman's ego had apparently found a playmate and that was all that seemed to matter. That is, until the next week, when, knowing I'd never skied before, he took me skiing.

MAYBE BECAUSE HEMINGWAY SKIED NORMAN felt he had to be good at it too, though I never had any desire to ski, and even when Monica and I took our two young sons snowboarding, neither of us even considered doing anything there ourselves, we were observing parents and nothing more. I don't doubt that this had something to do with my one experience skiing with Norman. I was visiting him in Stockbridge on a Saturday night in January 1975 when he suddenly announced that we were going skiing at Catamount, a ski resort in Hillside, New York, about a one-hour drive away. A lark, I believe he called it. I was game, though, it seemed like fun; after all, how hard could it be? But once there, after introducing me to an instructor who would show me the basics, he went off to the advanced slope, leaving me to "learn the basics," which apparently meant starting out on what was called the baby slope, along with, well, some kids so little they could barely stand up on their skis. I was indignant to the point of upset and angry. If I was tough enough to box with, I shouldn't be cast aside with ten-year-olds. When I asked about the slope off to our right, the instructor explained it was the intermediate slope, for much more experienced skiers. I didn't ask if there was a beginner's slope, fearing it would also involve children, and, believing I could handle something a little more advanced, I waited for the instructor to turn his back, and made my way over to the lift for this next slope. Once there, having no idea how to proceed, I studied all the skiers strapping themselves into their chairlifts, and, mimicking the man ahead of me in line, I got on the next chairlift, strapped myself in, positioned my skis between my legs the way he did, and suddenly found myself swaying high up in the air on a cable that was also swaying in the very cold and crisp air. Feeling empowered, if a little queasy, I got off when it stopped abruptly, jerking about, and, like everyone else, dropped my skis to the ground to step into them, except that, when I did it, they went flying off in either direction. The official who retrieved them for me asked politely if I needed further assistance, giving me a rather concerned and inquiring look. But I was determined to make the best of it, and, after mimicking everyone else in putting on my skis (the instructor at the baby slope was about to teach me that when I left), I slowly and clumsily made my way over to the edge, where I looked down the very steep slope at all the skiers gliding down the white earth in graceful patterns that seemed designed to make them come close to one another without ever colliding. Perhaps it was time, I thought, to turn around and confess my mistake and return to my rightful place on the baby slope? But several impatient-looking people were standing behind me and the idea of appearing cowardly and retreating was too embarrassing. How bad could things get, I told myself, I enjoyed a good sense of balance and even if I fell down a few times, how bad could that be? Norman would never know about it.

So, using the defense that I didn't know any better, I did what all us kids in the old neighborhood would do, I flung myself over the edge onto what appeared to be the beginning of an endless expanse of sheer white ice. Fighting the impulse to shut my eyes, I suddenly found myself heading straight down the slope without any sense or knowledge of how to do what everyone in front of me clearly knew how to do, a side-to-side movement Norman later explained was called traversing that allowed one to control not only their speed but their angle of descent. But every time I tried to move sideways, I nearly fell down and then, terrified, and not knowing what to do with my poles, one got stuck in the snow and became unattached from my wrist and flew out of my hand, nearly hitting a man skiing off to my left. And now, recognizing my complete ineptitude, everyone in front of me was trying to get out of my way, lunging forward and to the side, one or two falling down and cursing me, each and every one yelling instructions I couldn't or didn't want to hear. And then two patrol guys were suddenly on either side of me, yelling at me to fall down, just fall down, which I very much wanted to do, shifting my weight from side to side and lunging forward, but everything I did only increased my speed, which is when the guy to my left tried to knock my ski out from under me, while the one to my right bumped against me, hard, knocking my right ski off, which we all watched fly into the air, nearly hitting an older man frantically trying to escape. So now, skiing with one pole and one ski, going ever faster while the patrol guys continued to yell instructions at me, we all headed straight down toward a crowd of people standing at the bottom of the slope, watching us descend toward them as if out of a dream.

And then, maybe only a few feet from these now scattering people, one of the guards managed to knock me over, and I fell to the ground, my one ski flying off into the sky, and then rolled the rest of the way down the hill until I finally came to a stop in a large mound of snow, where Norman was standing, looking down at me. "Turn around and look at your handiwork," he said, pointing at the slope behind me, where a good number of bodies were strewn in various states of reconstitution and surrender, a few glaring down at me. "I have only one question," he said. "Why did you settle for this slope and not take on the advanced one?"

It wasn't a question that required an answer, and I didn't give him one.

A MAGIC ACT

The first time I almost met Elizabeth Bishop occurred in San Francisco in 1968, at the home of married poet friends who had studied with her in New York City some four or five years previously. I wasn't sure of the exact reason for this party, whether it was already planned and she surprised them with a visit, or whether it was designed to introduce her to their writer friends, though we were all made aware of the fact that she, Bishop, would be there.

She was sitting over in a corner of the living room, in a big, overstuffed Salvation Army armchair, a woman of fifty or so, handsome in a somewhat schoolmarmish way, her trim wavy brown haircut and collarless blue blouse and long gray skirt props, I thought, designed to underplay the fierce intellect and shy cunning behind her very charming, almost girlish smile. She was doing my friends a favor, no doubt, providing them with a boost in this tiny society of mostly transplanted New Yorkers, all of whom looked so pleased to be here, with her, in this tiny house on a hill in the Mission District whose living room windows all seemed to look out over other hills that appeared to be climbing the vibrant sky like so many steps in a stage setting designed for the benefit of only one person there. Yes, the party *was* for her, she and the young attractive woman with a very young child who was sitting at her side, both looking adoringly at her. They were a couple, my friends later explained, the young woman had been some kind of assistant or graduate student to Bishop at the University of Washington in Seattle, where Bishop was teaching, and there was also a young husband involved, they thought but weren't sure, who appeared to no longer be in the picture. Bishop, they said, had finished her teaching semester and was now headed back east, most likely with the young woman and her child. This was all stated in a whispered rush in a far corner of another room a very long time ago, but the young woman did appear to be the reason Bishop looked so happy, which is also, perhaps, the reason my friends so adamantly attempted at various times to introduce me to her. She had been a great source of inspiration in their lives and perhaps I too might benefit from knowing her. I tried, however unsuccessfully, to explain that I didn't want to intrude on Bishop's happiness and was more than happy to just hover near enough to eavesdrop and observe her every move, of which there were, in fact, few. Behaving, for the most part, like the royalty everyone there seemed to believe she was, she essentially never moved from her chair. When she wasn't talking to the young woman and her young child, she was laughing at something someone said, or graciously accepting a drink. It was a role she seemed not entirely comfortable with, and that she perhaps felt somewhat obligated to fulfill.

Once or twice, I considered introducing myself, perhaps by remarking on the view of hills and incoming fog, fog being a dependable source of conversation for us local Mission District dwellers. I lived only a few blocks away in an ancient duplex apartment that one had to pass through a kind of tunnel to reach, which, for a reason no one understood, was always filled with fog, the air mysteriously clean and crisp on either end, its single lightbulb forever unlit, and through which, sober or not, I'd run, especially at night, once passing a shrouded figure standing in a doorway, who whispered softly, "Good evening and good luck." I could tell her about this fog-encrusted passageway or my invisible neighbor Paddy Edgewood, who lived in the other part of the duplex, and whose accordion I often heard at night, but whose face I never once saw in the three years I lived next door—yes, I could tell her all this, it almost always got a good laugh, or I could just continue to stand there like a coat stand, tongue-tied and silent.

Which is when, as if to rescue me, the wife of my host friend came over to ask Bishop if there wasn't something she could do to improve her husband's mood—he was, in fact, sulking at his own birthday party (which it turned out to be)—since she, Elizabeth, was something of a magician, after all. Smiling generously, Bishop asked for a newspaper and, being given one, quickly tore off a page and began, with the alacrity and skill that seemed nothing less than miraculous, folding it into the figure of a bird. Yes, a life-sized, newspaper bird that actually looked as if it could fly of its own powers. We were all staring at her and it now, because it, this magical paper being, did seem to be coming to life before our very eyes. It was a performance unlike any I'd ever witnessed. And now, having finished creating it, she took a cigarette lighter out of her purse and, pausing to smile at her audience, called my friend over in a voice no larger, louder, or more commanding than that of a small girl. He, my friend, who had been standing nearby watching along with all the rest of us, now came over to stand obediently before her, as curious as he was perhaps concerned—what role, after all, could he possibly be playing in all this? Glancing around at her enraptured audience, she paused only to smile first at my friend and then at the paper bird, both of whom seemed anxious for the next act to commence, and then, with a snap of her thumb, she lit the lighter and then the bird, which seemed of its own volition to float up into the air, its wings aglow with fire. As if choreographed to do so, we all stepped back in unison, to see the paper bird hover high above her head, its tiny wings robustly flapping in what perhaps was a sudden breeze bestowed upon it and us by some indigenous god who just happened to be passing by and, like all the rest of us, became so enthralled as to forget wherever else had occupied her. Along with all the rest of us, my friend was laughing and clapping his hands, and then was dancing from foot to foot, as if he too had been set on fire and transformed into someone entirely new and happier.

I remember little of what followed, only that I could barely bring myself to look her way, fearing the slightest distraction might spoil the sheer exhilaration of the moment. And when I did glance at her, she was still sitting there, in her overstuffed chair, smiling a smile of pure contrition, as if she too, along with all the rest of us, was awe-struck by her own wizardry. Was this her expression after she completed writing "One Art" and was too exhausted by the effort to feel anything other than some small sense of wonder, and pride? In any case, she now had successfully completed her chore and could enjoy the results. My friend's mood, along with everyone else's, had been, for the foreseeable future, very much improved.

IN THE FALL OF 1979, my editor at Viking Press called to say that my first book of poems, *Like Wings*, had been nominated for a National Book Award, and, knowing my admiration for Elizabeth Bishop's poetry, she added that Bishop was one of the three judges. The book had just come out that fall and was, for the most part, well received, and I now had a part-time teaching job at NYU, so things were going okay, though I felt some frustration at being alone. I remember wondering what this would all mean, this kind of recognition. It might help me find a full-time teaching position, I thought, and maybe even a girlfriend. I was unsuccessful, however, in allowing myself to feel anything in particular about Bishop being one of the judges. Another judge was a friend of mine, the poet Michael Harper, who had befriended both Ralph Dickey and me, and there was a poem about Dickey in the book that I'd worked on for nearly five years—"The Gift"—of which he had seen several drafts, and I assumed he was the reason I'd been nominated for the award. It was even possible, given how these kinds of literary negotiations went, that Bishop didn't even like my book, or hadn't even read it. James Merrill's *Mirabell: Books of Number*, was also nominated and she and Merrill, as everyone knew, were close friends. He would most certainly win, and deservedly so. Just being mentioned in the same breath as Merrill was a high compliment. But thinking further about Bishop and my book seemed futile, and self-defeating.

But news about things like this gets around fast and within an hour or so friends were calling to congratulate me. All of them mentioned the same thing: that Elizabeth Bishop was one of the judges and what did I think about that. I said I was truly honored and changed the subject, at least in these conversations. Not so much in my mind. A lot was going on suddenly, reading offers and the kind of attention a young poet can only dream about, this being New York City, where fame can come as easily and swiftly as it leaves. The one thing that was constant, however, was my endless curiosity and internal debate about whether or not Bishop liked my book. I worried, for the most part, that she didn't, couldn't possibly, we were so different in background and bearing, I wrote about attending girlie shows, for God's sake, and possessing savage feelings, and Darwin, tortoises, and the Galápagos Archipelago, and a whole lot of love poems about various women, compared to her more elegant and sophisticated poems—why in the world would she like my work well enough to select it out of hundreds of poetry books published that year, it didn't seem to be even a remote possibility.

Even considering doing what just about all my friends were trying to convince me to do, which was write her and ask if she in any way had anything to do with my being nominated, was a terrible, truly awful idea. Yes, I knew my shitbird was going to town over this, my dreams were filled with my being trapped indefinitely in revolving doors and falling off subway platforms into oncoming trains, all and each with its particularly odious signature. And now, I was convinced, it wanted me to completely ruin whatever joy I might be feeling by writing her and receiving, most certainly, a response of silence.

Mainly to stop the torturous indecision, I finally decided to write her asking for a recommendation for a Guggenheim fellowship, which I truly wanted, and needed to help pay off my remaining student debt. So I wrote her a brief note asking her if she would be so kind as to allow me to use her name as a recommendation for a Guggenheim fellowship, mentioning the party in 1968 in San Francisco at the home of our mutual friends, where she had performed a magic act that still delighted me. I was pleased, I said, to be nominated for an award in which she was one of the judges. After a good number of drafts, my note was brief and casual sounding enough to sound reasonable to me. Reasonable in the sense that I wasn't really asking her for her opinion of my book, at least not outright. I remember addressing the envelope and placing a stamp in the nearly appropriate place on the envelope and walking down the stairs of my building and then down the hall and out to the street. I remember that it was a crisp late-September morning and that the flower boxes in many of the first-floor windowsills looked particularly splendid. I walked quickly and didn't hesitate in opening the lid of the mailbox and dropping the letter inside. I then went back home quickly and saluted myself with a shot of single-malt scotch that I'd been keeping for just such an occasion.

I don't remember how much later—four or five days, a week or two?—I received a postcard back from Miss Bishop, but suddenly it seemed as if she were in the room with me, performing yet another magic act:

LEWIS WHARF, OCTOBER 5TH, 1979

> *Dear Mr. Schultz: I am sorry to be so late in answering your note about the Guggenheim. It was forwarded, re-forwarded to Boston, and then when I finally got to Boston, I was sick for ten days or so.*
>
> *I hope this doesn't come too late. I'd be glad to have you use my name as a reference—so if this isn't too late, tell them to send me the forms.*
>
> *I did admire LIKE WINGS—in fact it was one of the few of the 100's of books one receives to read for the NBA that I actually <u>kept</u>.*
>
> *Sometime we must discuss NYU—perhaps later, when I'll be feeling more objective about it!*

With best wish—& good luck with the G!
[ELIZABETH BISHOP'S SIGNATURE]

I was overjoyed and, to my surprise, believed every word of it. Why would she lie? She didn't have to even answer me, let alone agree to write a recommendation for me. And I had heard rumors from colleagues about her brief and unpleasant tenure at NYU; when her name came up the subject was quickly changed. I was the first poet hired since her and was also met by some with a degree of skepticism. In fact, on my first day on the job, I found in my mailbox, along with everyone else's, a six-page single-spaced letter from an anonymous source outlining the changes my hiring would most certainly bring to the department, not the least of which would be creative types running through the halls emoting. To make sure I understood the meaning, I looked the word up: a gerund or present participle, it meant portraying emotion in a theatrical manner. Without doubt, however successfully, it's what writers and their students did, perform and display human emotion. And this prediction proved entirely accurate; within a year or two MFA students were in fact flavoring the halls in a highly charged manner. Yes, we would have things to discuss—perhaps a friendship would ensue. I kept standing up and sitting down, and then walking around my small apartment—she was ill, sick for ten days, and still she wrote me! But she liked my book, my poems, she wouldn't lie about that. It was a feeling unlike any I'd ever had. I had to tell someone, and I called my dear friend, the wonderful poet Grace Schulman, whose silence after I read her Bishop's card was alarming. I'd expected her to be overjoyed for me, having been one of the friends who had convinced me to write Bishop. When I asked what was wrong, she said something to the effect that she was sorry to have to tell me, but Bishop's obituary was in the *New York Times* that morning. She then asked me to tell her the date on Bishop's card, which was October 5. She had died on the sixth, Grace said, a day after writing and sending the card. It was a beautiful note, she said, which confirmed in no uncertain terms her admiration for my poetry.

I sat in that same black phony leather chair I'd sat in after I'd learned of my nomination. I sat staring at nothing in particular. Only a few moments before, I was as happy as I could ever remember being. A few moments that already seemed hours, days, weeks, years away. Was this just another of her magic acts, appearing so vibrantly alive one minute and so thoroughly absent the next? But she had gifted me with her words, words I would cherish the rest of my life. She was clearly sick when she wrote it, too ill to be writing letters to strangers, having to testify on their behalf. Too ill to be giving such precious last words.

I sat there a long time, remembering her magic act for my friend. The look on her face as the paper bird flew up into the air and everyone laughed. It seemed like only yesterday, *a yesterday I find almost impossible to lift.*

INDIAN WRESTLING

Though I always assumed it was my version of his own recklessness, the street kid who made up dangerous games and ignored the fateful consequences, that attracted Norman to me, it eventually became clear that despite his appreciation for what he deemed "my fearlessness," the sensitive and perhaps vulnerable poet in him also sought companionship, an attraction he would no doubt find difficult to admit to. These qualities, which he appreciated in others, didn't somehow fit into the comforting image he'd created for himself: that of a powerful man who would never back down from a fight, even, maybe especially, one he himself cultivated. It was the same image Hemingway found comfort in, that of the gladiator and matador, an image that to some degree belied the very element of their natures that wrote their most influential and, yes, beautiful work: their sensitivity. In other words, the poet in them. Hemingway's best work is his most powerfully felt, where the language becomes a thing unto itself, not a means to an end, not evidence of his intelligence or force of will, but an evocation of his love of the very process in which he was conveying everything he believed worthy of his undiluted attention: his passion for language. His inimitable lyricism is his openness, his embrace of the world at its most beautiful, and ugly. War and love and cowardice and honor were not only ideas but ideals, and sources of inspiration, and his keen sensitivity to language, his romance with the intimacy of his perceptions not only conveyed this passion, it was also its source. And yet Hemingway and Norman and so many other male writers of their times, and perhaps even ours, saw their sensitivity as unmanly. Indeed, because they saw the kind of delicate, nuanced, detailed sympathy required to write on this level as being feminine in nature, they couldn't acknowledge to themselves or others the very means or qualities of their originality and chose to align themselves with their more primitive instincts. In other words, their shitbirds despised their very source of inspiration and created personas that used self-loathing, booze, drugs, and a rejection of intimacy as weapons against what was quintessentially the poet in themselves.

Thus all the debilitating swagger in their lives and work, their unending war with the very nature of their brilliance, which they both perhaps saw as the price they had to pay for it. To read Hemingway's *A Moveable Feast* with his painterly, beautifully musical evocation of the cafés, streets, and famous painters and writers he knew as a young writer in the Paris of the 1920s, in which he turned nostalgia into poetry so lavishly emotional I couldn't read more than a few pages without feeling overwhelmed by the sheer lyricism of his language: "All of the sadness of the city came suddenly with the first cold rains of winter, and there were no more tops to the high white houses as you walked but only the wet blackness of the street and the closed doors of the small shops, the herb sellers, the stationery and the newspaper shops, the midwife—second class—and the hotel where Verlaine had died where I had a room on the top floor where I worked." Or the music of Norman's language in *An American Dream*: "Once, in a rainstorm, I witnessed the creation of a rivulet. The water had come down, the stream had begun in a hollow of earth the size of a leaf. Then it filled and began to flow. The rivulet rolled down the hill between some

stalks of grass and weed, it moved in spurts, down the fall of a
ledge, down to a brook. It did not know it was not a river."

My own struggle with the poet in me no doubt reflected a similar fear, that my need to celebrate, eulogize, and admit feelings of
inadequacy and self-contempt was a sign of weakness, most certainly in my father's eyes. According to my private system of belief,
a poet would never choke someone who was stealing from him,
which my father was so proud of doing; he would never strut about
in a rain dance of self-idolization, at least not the kind of poets that
I read and admired. Perhaps my being the poet in our friendship
freed Norman of any such obligation or conflict; anyone who used
their sensitivity as a sonar system for inspiration and consolation
was an interesting companion, even though it wasn't a quality to
boast about or publicize. Is this why Norman said to me more than
once, usually apropos of nothing, that a lack of humanity in his
work was the reason he would never win the Noble Prize? Though
it seemed only right that he should consider himself a candidate
for such acclaim—the ambition behind his invention of New Journalism, his ever-expanding capacity for critical analysis of every
important social, intellectual, and political event of his time, from
his book-length consideration of the Apollo 11 moon landing to the
American enshrinement of a sex goddess, Marilyn Monroe, and
most certainly his *Executioner's Song*, in which the very nature of
violence and self-violation is laid bare by a poetry that uses language to celebrate the very things it's excoriating—he seemed all
too aware of what was lacking in his suitability for such an award.
The very qualities that seemed to bring him so much public attention, his torturous and metaphysical self-examination and somewhat primitive inclination toward violence, didn't exactly promote
the kind of sensitivity that he was referring to by "a lack of humanity." Sensitivity was for nice Jewish boys from Brooklyn, or poets

from Rochester, not fierce warriors and internationally recognized litterateurs. The poet in him didn't run for mayor, drink himself unconscious, look for fights, and exchange one love for another, and most certainly didn't repeatedly try to sabotage our friendship and push me away.

My unending commentary about everything that came my way must've been entertaining to him, even, and maybe especially, when he didn't like what I felt about something he said or did. An instance of this is the night he called me at Yaddo, where I was a resident, to ask me to lie to Carol Stevens, the woman he was living with, should she call me, which he suspected she would, about his new girlfriend, Norris Church. I was to tell her that Norris was my girlfriend and that I, not he, had been staying with her in his Brooklyn Heights apartment. This after he'd evicted me from that very place because I wouldn't stay there with her, as he proposed, and chose to leave and stay with friends, even though he'd promised to let me stay there until I found a place of my own in Manhattan.

All this began the Friday night in January 1976 when he brought her to his Brooklyn Heights pad, where I was staying, to meet me and then have dinner together. Norris, who became his sixth and final wife, was a splendidly tall and beautiful young woman more than twenty-five years his junior. They'd met at a party in Russellville, Arkansas, he said, where he was visiting friends and she was from, and given the way they were looking at each other, they were obviously in love. Even while talking to me he couldn't take his eyes off her, a trick that reminded me of a ventriloquist, maybe because I was beginning to feel somewhat like a dummy. At dinner, at a restaurant with a view of the East River that was a few blocks away from his place, I recounted my many frustrating experiences looking for the kind of apartment in Greenwich Village that I couldn't afford. Though there was nothing wrong with the Upper West Side, where there were apartments I could afford, I had my heart set on living in the Village. I was never practical, especially when I needed and attempted to be, and my adventures apartment-hunting were funnier than I'd realized, apparently, because they both were highly entertained by my stories of near misses and crazy landlords. One apartment on Bank Street, I said, that I had been given a key for and was supposed to be empty, had been turned into a brothel, where I was invited inside and offered a free massage for not telling the landlord what I found there. I refused to say what I chose to do, though, but as far as I could tell, they remained in business. Another place on West Fourth Street was filled with birds, mostly parrots, which the tenant, who was in the process of being evicted, rented out to various other ornithophiles through ads in the *Village Voice*; the tenant, an ex-priest who wrote books on wildlife conservation, offered me a free parrot if I took the place and let him stay there until he found somewhere to place his fifteen birds. The stink was driving other tenants to leave, the landlord confided in me. And then there was the much-bandaged-up super on Horatio Street who couldn't get out of bed to show me the apartment I came to see, who offered to bake me free birthday cakes for as long as I lived there if I didn't tell the landlord about his condition; he was a baker by trade, he said, and had been in a motorcycle accident. It was all great fun, with Norman going on about a recent prize fight he was writing an article about and Norris telling us about her adventures in Manhattan, where she'd never been before meeting Norman. Fun, that is, until I began to understand what the evening was really about, which was her meeting, and perhaps evaluating, both the apartment and me.

After dinner Norris asked me if I would like to see a catalog of glossy photos of her as a model, and Norman looked on with pride as she turned the pages, commenting along with her on the various fashion photographers who took the photos. Their interest was obviously greater than mine, I knew nothing and cared less about this sort of thing, but I politely played along until we came to the last few pages of the book, which were mostly nude photos of her. I'd seen my share of *Playboy* nudes as a kid, but not with any of the models sitting next to me. Norman's commentary continued even though it was probably obvious that I could barely force myself to glance at them. And when this part of the showcase was finally over, Norris excused herself and went off to the ladies' room, as if it was all rehearsed beforehand. Feeling set up, I also wanted to excuse myself and leave, but Norman was explaining that he'd promised to let her stay at his place and, knowing I couldn't afford to stay anywhere else while I looked for a place, and not wanting to kick me out, he'd given her the choice of staying there with me, if she liked me, that is. I should be pleased to know, he said, that, while I went to the bar earlier, she'd said yes. She liked me. Though it was obviously intended as a compliment, I didn't feel flattered in the least. The pages of nude photos lay open before me and, trying to avoid looking at them, I said no, that wouldn't work for me. Which made him laugh and say he knew I would say that. Though if he did, I thought, why did he have to put us all through this?

The walk back to his place, where I would stay that night and that night only, alone, seemed to take forever. I moved in with friends the next day, going from one friend to another for two weeks, until I finally found a place on Jane Street that I could almost afford. And since my new apartment wouldn't be ready for nearly a month, I then went to Yaddo, which I'd applied to months before, and where Norman called me one night while I was at dinner. The phone booths were in the lobby outside the dining hall and a writer, who'd left to make a phone call and answered the call, now stood in the entrance, loudly announcing to the room at large in the kind of raspy singsong voice one hears in musical comedy that "Norman Mailer wants to speak with Mr. Philip Schultz, if he's available." Though this kind of public announcement was bad manners here, where the identity of the caller is usually whispered in someone's ear, this particular resident apparently believed Mailer's identity was too noteworthy to keep private. The fact that John Cheever was in attendance in the room (he would pretty much come and go as he pleased while the rest of us applied half a year in advance and often didn't get invited) and was sitting at the table next to mine, staring in my direction for the first time, didn't exactly lessen my embarrassment. I wasn't ashamed of knowing Norman, of course, but didn't enjoy advertising the fact. It also didn't help that a second idiot would later ask if I'd paid the first idiot to make this announcement.

When I got to the phone booth, Norman sounded panicked, as if he'd been holding his breath until I got there. He had a great favor to ask of me, he said. Should Carol call me from Stockbridge, which he was pretty sure she would, I should tell her it was I and not he who'd been staying at his Brooklyn place with Norris. Without saying how she'd found out about Norris, he said he'd just gotten off the phone with Carol, who was very angry, and, not knowing what else to do, he told her that I was Norris's boyfriend and had been living with her at his place. He hoped I didn't mind but he'd also told her that I was at Yaddo.

It all roared past me in one ugly swoop; I was supposed to lie to someone I liked very much, someone who'd been warm and welcoming to me many times when I visited them in Stockbridge, someone who, on more than one occasion, I'd heard sing jazz at a local hotel cabaret. Well, I told him, I didn't like the idea of lying to someone I liked, I didn't care for it at all.

Expecting this to end our friendship, I sat there silently reading all the carved signatures, many of them the names of writers I recognized and admired—would I now be asked to leave Yaddo, too? Why couldn't I just do him a favor and lie to her? He'd certainly done enough favors for me.

After an excruciatingly long silence, he tried to make light of it and gave me a new nickname, Rabbi Schultz. I was Talmudic, he laughed, a real rabbi. He then got off the phone, having urgent matters to attend to now. But it didn't end our friendship, as I found out only a few days later, when he again called me there, this time asking for Rabbi Schultz, probably just to get even.

ANOTHER EXAMPLE OF THIS KIND of sabotage is the night Norman set up an Indian wrestling contest between me and José Torres, the light-heavyweight boxing champion of the world.

I always possessed a good sense of balance, it wasn't easy to knock me down at any street game and I once scored high in a state contest for being able to lift my body off the ground by balancing my weight on my hands, my knees resting on my elbows, for several long, agonizing minutes. This ability made me good at all kinds of sports, though Indian wrestling was something I excelled at through college. If I wanted to feel good about myself, I would challenge someone much bigger than me to a bout and then strut about like a peacock. In my freshman year at the University of Louisville, I helped pay my tuition by writing papers for the football team, the Division I Cardinals, that played and sometimes won titles in the NCAA Atlantic Coast Conference. I lived on the same dorm floor and would charge five bucks for an A, three for a B plus, and a dollar for a C, in any subject, knowing if I and they did well, I'd get a nice tip. My writing was good enough to impress even, or maybe especially, when I didn't have any idea what I was writing about, which meant just about every subject except for English.

The players, all twice my size, not only didn't mind paying me, but they also kind of adopted me as their mascot. If anyone looked askance at me, they would have what they called a little talk with them. Yes, the football team was my personal squad of bodyguards and I would sometimes eat with them in the cafeteria, all of which lasted until one of the coaches began to inquire what their fascination with me was all about. But for a while, it was heaven, and to enlarge their regard I would challenge one or two to a contest of Indian wrestling, contests that most of the time I won. Their size was my advantage, they had no idea what I was doing to win but loved the idea that someone my size, who was "smart," could beat them at anything that required physical prowess. None of them ever caught on that my only trick was to use their weight and confidence against them.

Which served me well with Norman Mailer, too, who never stopped trying to beat me, just once. It's a contest primarily of balance, in which the contestants face each other, planting their front foot side by side and, after bracing their back leg and foot behind them for balance, lock right hands and then try to force their opponent to move his back foot off the ground. Beating Norman wasn't all that hard. He was strong, very strong, but I knew how to shift my weight and outmaneuver him, and, to some degree, use his own stubborn determination against him. And then one Saturday night, after I'd driven up to Stockbridge from Cambridge with a lady friend to a big Fourth of July party he was throwing, he came looking for me as soon as we parked in front of his house to say he'd already challenged a friend of his to one of my leg-wrestling matches, that it should be great fun. The idea sounded terrible, like a public spectacle I wanted no part of. But Norman was insistent, his friend was outside on the patio and there were a lot of well-known boxing friends there, like Don King, and he wanted to, well, show me off.

What he didn't say was that they were already betting, and he'd put a hundred bucks on me. The woman I brought was a feminist academic I'd met at the MacDowell Colony retreat that summer and who wanted to come even though I'd warned her about the kind of macho atmosphere she'd find here. She was intrigued perhaps in the way an anthropologist might be in visiting a primitive civilization she'd only read about in books. Norman had never before greeted me with this kind of enthusiasm, so I knew something was up, and I reluctantly followed him through the house onto the backyard patio, where I suddenly found myself being introduced to José Torres, the light-heavyweight champion of the world.

I'd actually met him before at Norman's Brooklyn Heights pad, and found him to be an extremely warm and funny man, a Puerto Rican whose Peek-a-Boo style of boxing was something he himself often displayed for fun and had once tried to show me how to position myself in, with my body bent to the side and both raised fists covering my face. But the man I was now facing, dressed in a bright blue sports jacket and black pants, didn't look at all warm or funny. He was pouting, in fact, looking me over and pouting. Who did this little shit that Norman was bragging so much about think he was, is what I guessed this expression meant. Then he smiled, handed his glass to someone standing next to him, and in an accent I struggled to understand, said, "So you're the tough guy who can't be beat, eh?"

The woman I was with whispered in my ear, "Let's get out of here, this minute, really!"

We now seemed to be standing in the middle of an impromptu boxing ring of glaring faces, many angling to get a better look. Norman, who had been standing next to me a moment ago, was suddenly nowhere to be seen. While José continued to glare at me. Well, I told myself, it was only a game of leg wrestling, what could I lose, a little dignity? He was powerfully built, only a little taller but a lot heavier and all muscle. I knew I couldn't move him an inch, no matter how agile I was. And now, with everyone so eager to see what they probably assumed would be a massacre, I just wanted to get it over with. If I survived, I would let Norman know what I thought of all this, and maybe never see him again.

And then Norman was next to me, whispering something in my ear I couldn't make out, and yanking at my arm. Before I knew what was happening, I was being pulled through the crowd and into the house, my lady friend, looking relieved, hurrying to keep up with us. Inside the dining room, in a pantry, he hurriedly explained that a friend of José's mistress had been killed in a car accident in Puerto Rico earlier that day and he was in no mood to get beaten at anything. A mutual friend had just pulled Norman aside and told him, he said. "You beat him, and I think you will, and he'll probably kill you. It's all my fault, I had no idea, just thought it'd be fun, he's always such a sweetheart, really."

I was ordered to go upstairs to the attic room to hide while he would try to come up with some excuse—it was where we would spend the night anyway, he added—but we couldn't come back down until we heard from him. I shouldn't worry, he would take care of things. All I could think to say was that we hadn't eaten yet and were hungry. He and my lady friend both looked at me as if I was a madman. He was busy saving my life and I was worrying about eating?

Frightened and confused, we spent a good part of the rest of the evening in hiding. I never would've beaten him, I told myself, so there was nothing to worry about. And I should be flattered that Norman held me in such high regard. Yes, flattered, and relieved, I told myself, knowing I'd avoided what could've been a fateful confrontation. But, of course, my shitbird got the last word: now everyone knew what a phony and coward I was, first bragging about being unbeatable and then running off to hide. The fact that I did neither didn't seem to matter. Only the poet and fiction writer in me remained silent, perhaps too confused, finally, to even have an opinion.

There was another magician I was impressed with and actually met and even became friends with during my time in Cambridge, one whose very different magic act was in many ways just as mesmerizing and original as Elizabeth Bishop's. Denise Levertov was in Cambridge at the same time as Bishop, and though I often wondered if they ever met and knew each other—how could they not have, two women poets of international renown living so close together? But I never once saw them together or heard anyone mention both in the same sentence. Though I knew Denise and Adrienne Rich were good friends, when I once mentioned Bishop to Levertov, with whom I became friends quite early and easily during my time there, I remember only that if I even mentioned Elizabeth's name Denise quickly changed the subject and I understood not to mention her again. Denise knew, I thought, of my admiration for Bishop and, if she held any negative views, would've known better than to have said anything against her to me. They were very different kinds of poets, after all, in many ways nearly polar opposites. Elizabeth's more restrained and indirect approach to autobiographical subject matter served what she no doubt saw as her aesthetic mission, while Denise's more liberal, political, and, in a sense, egalitarian approach seemed willing to sacrifice everything to what she saw as the common good, or moral edification, of her audience. It's not hard to imagine how Bishop would react to a poem as blunt and dramatically personal as Denise's "Mad Song," from *Relearning the Alphabet*, published in 1970:

> My madness is dear to me.
> I who was almost always the sanest among my friends,
> one to whom others came for comfort,
> now at my breasts (that look timid and ignorant,
>> that don't look as if milk had flowed from them,
>> years gone by)
> cherish a viper.
>> Hail, little serpent of useless longing
> that may destroy me,
> that bites me with such idle
> needle teeth.
>
> I who am loved by those who love me
> for honesty,
> to whom life was an honest breath
>> taken in good faith,
> I've forgotten how to tell joy from bitterness.
>
> Dear to me, dear to me,
> blue poison, green pain in my mind's veins.
> How am I to be cured against my will?

Though I loved this poem and its very vulnerable, authentic, and excited persona, it's hard to imagine Bishop ever opening a poem with "My madness is dear to me" and then ending it with such a cry for help as "How am I to be cured against my will?" To be a serious reader of Bishop's poetry one learns quickly, as with a friend of some remove, what not to say or ask of her. There are many dissimilarities, certainly, between these two very different poets, though the similarities may be even more interesting. Both wanted very much to be understood clearly, emphatically, knew exactly what they were trying to say and what they were asking of their readers, and, perhaps most importantly, understood how far they were willing to go to be understood and appreciated. Neither wanted to be associated with any particular school of poetry or aesthetic approach (Denise was early on, with the Black Mountain School, along with Robert Creeley and Robert Duncan, though that changed quickly, I think), and though both dealt powerfully with their femininity neither cared to be seen as a feminist. And they each preferred personas that were as impassioned as they were confident of their aesthetic. But Levertov is so much more forthright and provocative, in the sense that—in the Marshall McLuhan lingo of the day—her message was the medium, or at least as important, unlike Bishop, who forever honored the medium of poetry and literature above all. To Denise, poetry, however sacred, served humanity by emphasizing and illuminating injustice wherever encountered, injustice being a credo too essential to be asked to take a back seat to any other concern or issue.

Her father was a Russian Hasidic Jew who converted to Christianity after moving to England, where he became an Anglican pastor; her mother was Welsh and homeschooled her and her sister, Olga, and apparently loved poetry enough to read it and a good portion of English literature to them each night. But the role William Carlos Williams played in her political and poetic thinking is apparent in so much of her work and life. His love of the plain-spoken American idiomatic directness—"no ideas but in things," meaning real things or objects rather than abstract ideas—is obvious in her every poem and essay, and her strict Judeo-Christian principles about justice and showing compassion for the less fortunate was certainly influenced by the concern he showed others as a physician driving around the back roads of New Jersey, treating the needy and the dispossessed. Near the end of a very long book-length poem, *Staying Alive*, in her 1971 book, *To Stay Alive*, she says as much to herself as her reader:

> Your being, a fiery stillness
> is needed to TRANSFORM
> the dogs.
>
> And Bet said to me:
> Get down into your well,
>
> it's your well
>
> go deep into it
>
> into your own depth as into a poem.

Yes, we must go deeply into our well, which is a commonly shared human well, as into the depth of each poem. And she was, in her person, as well as in her work, "a fiery stillness." A stillness and descent one can easily enough sense in Williams's great long poem, *Paterson*:

> —Say it, no ideas but in things—
> nothing but the blank faces of the houses
> and cylindrical trees
> bent, forked by preconception and accident—
> split, furrowed, creased, mottled, stained—

secret—into the body of light!

. . . .

The descent

            made up of despairs

                and without accomplishment

realizes a new awakening :

             which is a reversal

of despair.

      For what we cannot accomplish, what

is denied to love,

     what we have lost in the anticipation—

             a descent follows,

endless and indestructible

This reversal of despair is the passion, if not mission, of both these poets, a mission I can of course find also in Bishop's work. The body of light to be found deep in one's well, and in the depths of a poem, is also most certainly there in the work of all three.

But unlike with Bishop, getting to know Denise was easy and natural. We were both teaching at Tufts University, in and around 1974, I, one section of freshman composition, while Denise was their writer-in-residence, a position of some esteem and attention. Nearly overnight everyone in the area knew she was there in the same way everyone knew Bishop was enthroned a few miles away at Harvard, or later, when her teaching at Harvard was made more permanent, at Lewis Wharf. Since Lowell was mostly off teaching in England, they were the reigning poetic royalty in the area. (Adrienne Rich was at Brandeis then, though her presence, as far as I knew, wasn't as keenly felt.) Denise seemed to be everywhere at once, shepherding political and literary events, just as she had in 1968 when I returned to San Francisco and she was at the epicenter of all the hell that was breaking out at SF State and in Berkeley, where she taught. Her powerful 1967 collection of antiwar poems and elegies for her sister, Olga, *The Sorrow Dance*, and *Relearning the Alphabet* in 1970, with its poems dealing with People's Park, pretty much cemented her reputation as fine poet and antiwar activist. In fact, she was so closely identified with People's Park, the event that galvanized the various and conflicting ideologies of the New Left on and off the Berkeley and SF State campuses, she seemed as much a leader of the antiwar resistance as Ginsberg, Tom Hayden, and Jerry Rubin themselves. There she was, at just about every protest, rabble-rousing and prancing about various impromptu stages with a mike in one fist and a list of grievances or poetry book in the other, with her short brown hair and dark eyes and constantly swerving body language, every inch the daughter of Hasidic wild dancing mixed with Anglican docility, performing a magic act as hypnotic as it was proselytizing, a spectacle that raised the already high pitch of anger and indignation to one of vision and inspiration.

This from "Staying Alive":

(October '68–May '69)

    I

Revolution or death. Revolution or death.
Wheels would sing it
                    but railroads are obsolete,
we are among the clouds, gliding, the roar
a toneless constant.
                Which side are you on?
Revolution, of course. Death is Mayor Daley.

Which side are you on?—revolution, of course! All of which seemed to be happening everywhere around me every day when I was an undergraduate at SF State, which in 1968 became a major battleground of antiwar activism. We all, students and professors alike, seemed to be spending most of our time dodging nightsticks and getting locked up in school buses, which were occasionally left or misplaced, sometimes overnight, in vacant parking lots. The then governor Ronald Reagan personally hated the SF State campus almost as much as he hated UC Berkeley with its People's Park, which he considered "a haven for communist sympathizers, protesters and sexual deviants." His proclamation that only police and military force would cure things was famous throughout the state, if not country —"If it takes a bloodbath, let's get it over with, no more appeasement." Denise and others took him at his word and returned force with force. On the SF State campus, with its army of antiwar activists, he sent in the National Guard again and again, and when she wasn't at one campus, she was at the other any number of times. I returned from Iowa to this "bloodbath," and once, during a protest, one of my writing teachers, and friends, George Price, who was much taller than I, stepped in front of a police club that was aimed at my head, and, since the infirmary was filled and there was nowhere else to take the injured, he received many stitches while lying on the grass, smiling up at me. I don't remember what I'd called this particular policeman's mother, though he apparently took it personally, all of which is to say that to stand out in any meaningful way amid all this constant pandemonium was no small feat, but whenever Denise took the stage everyone noticed. Usually, after four or five speakers at most of these rallies, one had heard more than enough, but her passion was both genuine and infectious, as all those roaring crowds demonstrated. What she wrote in her prose book about poetry and poets, *The Poet in the World*, sums up her ideas perfectly: "Only revolution can now save that earthly life, that miracle of being, which poetry conserves and celebrates." No one would ever accuse Elizabeth Bishop of making so large and "revolutionary" a claim. (Though perhaps a case could be made for some sense of revolution in her poems—they did play their part in shaping American poetry.)

Denise and I met on the Tufts campus, at a political event, and before long we were getting together after our classes and having coffee together in Cambridge, where she took me to lunch on my twenty-ninth birthday, giving me three of her signed books and saying she was certain she would be holding one of mine before too long. This may have been wishful thinking on her part, because, though she asked to see my poetry, I hadn't yet shown her any. It wasn't that I was insecure about my poetry but once again the novelist in me was creating its own egotistical upheaval and I was somehow smart enough to never mention my fiction writing to her—as far as she was concerned, I looked, acted, and talked like a poet and therefore, like it or not, that's what I was, a poet. Mitch Goodman, her husband at the time, was a novelist and antiwar activist on a grand level. He helped organize the antiwar protest at the Pentagon that Mailer wrote about in *Armies of the Night* and was one of those charged with conspiracy in the Boston Five trials in 1967, and though I met him only a few times at dinner at their house in Somerville, his intense intellect and brooding political anxieties were obvious from the start; as was the fact that they, Denise and he, weren't exactly getting along. This was obvious at one of our dinners when Denise read aloud a draft of my poem "Like Wings," which was about the end of my relationship with Marie, because, I thought, she found the very idea of my relationship with Marie somewhat, well, amusing, if not hilarious.

She'd heard me read the poem at a reading and asked to see a copy. The fact that the poem was taking nearly as long to complete—its early drafts dated back to 1971 when we were living in Kalamazoo—as our relationship had lasted and that Marie herself read and commented on various drafts only added to her curiosity about it. Knowing it wasn't finished, and that she probably wouldn't take no for an answer, I showed it to her mainly just to get it over with, not expecting of course that she'd read it aloud at the dinner table. It was obvious from Mitch's expression that he didn't care at all for the poem. It was Denise's opinion I wanted, but she was now staring only at Mitch. Well, she asked finally, what did he think? He thought it romantic, self-indulgent, and "confessional," a word that, because of Sylvia Plath's and Anne Sexton's fame, not to mention that of their teacher, Robert Lowell, had many detractors. For a reason I didn't bother to wonder about, the only word I minded was "romantic." Being called self-indulgent and confessional was fine, apparently, but what was so romantic about a love poem? He couldn't answer a question I didn't actually ask, but he did ask why it was taking so long to write, and before I could think of a reason worth saying out loud—the truth was I had no idea whatsoever—Denise was answering him for me, saying something to the effect that in writing so many drafts over so long a time I was perhaps managing to develop a style and persona that would help me write my other poems. I liked this idea tremendously, of course, and could've hugged her for saying it. She then added that she often thought of Williams when she wrote, and that his rather strident personality—he could be churlish in disagreeing with anything having to do with poetry—had certainly influenced the way she thought about and then actually wrote her poems. It in fact wasn't hard recognizing Williams's voice even in some of the things she said to me, innocuous things like why I appeared to have stopped eating (I was losing a lot of weight then) or did Marie have anything to do with my choice of clothes (though I did have a habit of wearing clothes to the point where they finally surrendered and slowly unraveled, she wasn't being critical, I didn't think, so much as objectively curious). Mitch didn't say much after this, though he did seem to concur with the notion that the struggle with one poem could impact the outcome of what was written later. I thought of but managed not to mention the fact that Bishop had taken some sixteen years to write "The Moose," a poem that influenced not only her own later poems but those of most accomplished poets I knew.

In any case, "Like Wings" was published in the *New Yorker* two years later, in February 1977, and received, according to Howard Moss, their poetry editor, a record number of letters, many of which, ironically, were from women offering various forms of consolation and advice on my future love decisions. But my first real intimation of its future was the disturbance it caused at Denise's house over dinner that night. Though Denise didn't really say what she thought of the poem, she did comment on a stanza she found particularly curious:

> There are hours when the future gives up all hope
> & stops in the middle of busy streets
> & doesn't care. But think of the distance we have come,
> the hands which have wound us.
> There will be others.

Had I actually reached a point where I'd given up all hope, or was I being dramatic, she asked. I said I was very down and close to giving up, and Mitch wondered if I'd worried that so personal a confession might strike others as being indulgent, especially during times like these (the Watergate hearings were taking place). Denise then defended a poet's right (not mine in particular, but any poet's right) to write love poetry even during times of political upheaval, adding that perhaps such times may even be the best time to write it. Making *Doctor Zhivago* a love story in the midst of the Russian Revolution didn't seem to hurt Pasternak, after all. It soon became clear, at least to me, that whatever argument they were having had little to do with my poem, or me. They in fact separated the following year and were divorced not long afterward; yes, it was sad that a poem about the pain of separation should cause an argument about the very same thing.

FOR A REASON I STILL don't understand, Denise once insisted on accompanying me as I did errands in Cambridge, mostly, I assumed, to get away from everything else, maybe especially whatever she was working on (and she was always working on something, leaving over twenty poetry books when she died in Seattle in 1997 at the age of seventy-four; a far different volume from the eighty poems and four collections Bishop published during her lifetime). And it was after one of these errands, to my dry cleaner, that she asked, with genuine curiosity and affection, if I enjoyed complicating the most simple and straightforward transactions to the point of utter confusion or was I not aware I was doing it? Did I notice, for instance, that by the time I'd finished giving instructions on how I wanted my clothes cleaned, asked several questions about their procedures, and then argued about the costs, the young woman attendant looked completely exasperated and defeated? No, I told her, I hadn't noticed. It seemed a pretty typical interaction to me, the kind my father, my grandma, and most certainly Jake would have with almost everyone, I remembered. As simple a thing as a haircut for my father and an ordinary visit to the kosher bakery for my grandma, I told her, could end up involving everyone present in an endless melee that would somehow churn up politics, religion, personal myths, and nostalgia for the dead and the hereafter, not to mention wondering why one bothered ever leaving home in the first place. In fact, I never understood why my grandma wanted me along (she may have just wanted a witness) but almost every time, a fight broke out at the bakery, like the Friday morning when a Romanian Jewish woman I'd thought was her friend asked her in Yiddish, which I could understand, where she got her hat, she herself had always wanted one just like it. It was big with a furry knotted ball on top and the woman was obviously trying to compliment her but suddenly Grandma was shouting at her in Lithuanian or Polish or maybe Russian (when she got angry she sometimes spoke four or five languages at once, confusing even herself), and the woman, obviously insulted, yanked her own furry hat off and threw it at Grandma, who picked it up, spat on it, and then tossed it over her shoulder, hitting another woman, named Mrs. Tillem, whom no one ever liked, right in the face. Suddenly everyone, including the owner and his wife behind the counter, was screaming at everyone else, in Yiddish so they would all understand exactly what they were saying. I never knew why we ever went there in the first place, because we often came home empty-handed, with Grandma muttering under her breath for days afterward. And I never again saw the hat she was wearing; she probably buried it in the backyard along with every other indignity she'd been made to suffer.

After a while, I said, I dreaded going with any of them almost anywhere where other human beings might be found. Denise was suddenly laughing so hard we had to stop walking and find a place to sit down, which wasn't always easy in Harvard Square, where the constant onrush of students, tourists, workers, and ideas could be overwhelming. She later mentioned this exchange on several occasions, each time finding it even more bizarre and amusing. Apparently, I went through life complicating just about everything, confusing the superficial with the essential and simplifying the impossible, without even being aware of it. If there was a lesson here for me, I failed miserably to understand it, other than the fact that Denise obviously found me amusing, and to some degree sympathized with my constant sense of confusion. At times, it seemed a kind of religion, or act of faith, to me, she once pointed out. If I was amusingly confused, fine and good, I decided.

After her divorce, Denise went off to Yaddo to finish a book, while I was busy teaching full-time at the University of Massachusetts at Boston and thinking seriously about moving to New York City. She wrote around then asking me if I could drive up to Saratoga Springs and pick her up when her stay was done, and then we could drive back together and have our laughs again. I wrote back saying that as much fun as that seemed there were any number of reasons I couldn't. My car, a very old VW wagon, wouldn't make it, and I was busy teaching, etcetera. The truth is I didn't want to go and wasn't all that sure why. Maybe I was coming down with another case of perplexity and being of service to anyone just seemed too complicated and exhausting. In any case, as much as such a trip would no doubt prove memorable, my stay in Cambridge seemed ready to be over with, my life there already a thing of the past, and I was determined to move my bewilderment farther south. I moved to New York the following spring and though I thought of her often, and continued to follow her work, we did manage to lose touch after that, especially after she returned to California to teach at Stanford and I became, well, entrenched in my New York City life. The war and its revolutions were well over by now, though the madness that was so dear to both of us continued uninterrupted for some time to come.

VOICES VEILED AND UNVEILED

W hen I first came to New York I survived for nearly two years on part-time jobs teaching poetry in the surrounding elementary schools for the Poets in the Schools program and doing clerical work at Poets & Writers, each a wonderfully generous society that offered me the company of kindred spirits and ports of entry into the larger creative society I was seeking. And then I was asked to guest-teach a private writing workshop set up by a group of writers who'd just lost their teacher and liked poems of mine they'd seen in the *New Yorker*. These writers, my new students, were an odd and interesting mix: some had recently graduated from college; others worked in publishing and insurance, taught high school and college English; two commuted from New Jersey and Long Island; and one or two had MFAs but had stopped writing for a longer period than they cared to talk about. What we all now had in common was a keen desire to be poets and writers, serious writers. People came and went, as we all seemed to be constantly moving, and though it's hard to say exactly why the basic class held together, one thing was clear: I now had the opportunity to experiment with my ideas about persona writing that I'd been developing since my first teaching job at Kalamazoo College in 1972, when, desperate to get my freshman students to stop using in their stories and poems the autobiographical "I" they used in their letters and diaries (and that I ironically continued to use in my fiction), I asked them to imitate the "I" of Walt Whitman's *Song of Myself*, because, I explained, his narrator was so lush with attitude and pride, so generous and abundant toward everything human, even a touch of such magnitude and largess could inspire in them a larger and more engendering interest in the world beyond their immediate lives. Here are a few lines from Whitman's luscious praise of the living self:

> Walt Whitman, a kosmos, of Manhattan the son,
> Turbulent, fleshy, sensual, eating, drinking and breeding,
> No sentimentalist, no stander above men and women or apart
>   from them,
> No more modest than immodest.
> . . . .
> Through me many long dumb voices,
> Voices of the interminable generations of prisoners and slaves,
> Voices of the diseas'd and despairing and of thieves and dwarfs,
> Voices of cycles of preparation and accretion,
> And of the threads that connect the stars, and of wombs and of
>   the father-stuff,
> And of the rights of them the others are down upon,
> Of the deform'd, trivial, flat, foolish, despised,
> Fog in the air, beetles rolling balls of dung.
>
> Through me forbidden voices,
> Voices of sexes and lusts, voices veil'd and I remove the veil,
> Voices indecent by me clarified and transfigur'd.
> . . . .
> I believe in the flesh and the appetites.

("SONG OF MYSELF," SECTION 24, *LEAVES OF GRASS*
[NEW YORK: MODERN LIBRARY COLLEGE EDITIONS,
1950], 43–44)

It wasn't until many years later, while working on the last poem in my second book of poems, *Deep Within the Ravine*, that I realized this was exactly the kind of generosity of spirit I hoped to convey in the final poem of my book. It was a time of disappointment and self-denial, when nothing seemed to be working, and I knew that the part of me that wanted to give up was well represented in the long and dark title poem and I wanted to end the book on a more positive note. I was in a great funk after yet another failed novel and bad relationship came to an end and I wanted to celebrate, if not praise, what I believed was still worthwhile about myself when so little seemed to be praiseworthy. I wanted a voice that could speak for the strength I found in Whitman to withstand the forces of darkness within myself. I realized immediately whose persona was needed and then was surprised when the tone of voice came so spontaneously.

THE QUALITY

There is in each body something splendid, I think,
        a kind of sheltering, say, the suit of
hours we wear like weather, or instinct striking
        the spine's cold accordion, that ripening
of reflex that is the mind's appetite for testimony,
        yes, in darkness there is strength hoarded

against damage, say, the flowering of desire imprinted
        in the infant's smile as it awakens out of

its dream of creation, I mean pain is not sentiment only,
        but a fierce healing, like light rebuilding,
out of darkness, our original boundaries, yet something
        is lost in the growing, yes, the greater

the gift the more troubling the sleep, like lovers lost
        in the body's cold spin, we are naked
within the shell of our temperament, beings greater in
        mystery after violation, yes, like strips
of horizon, the spirit unwinds its gift of a single life,
        moment by moment, say, that quality of love

that is not physical, but sensed, like vision burning
        in the eye's garden, yes, once again spring
arrives after winter's long ash & I accept despair's
        selfish fruit as the fermenting of wonder
that springs out of everything lost & dying, say,
        that furthering of instinct, which, like

the spider's ambition to infinitely extend its life
        another inch of light, glistens like rain
over the attic window where I sat as a boy entranced
        with the radiance of first longing, yes,
a quality so distinctly human we glow like light burning
        over all the fire-struck windows of our lives.

Whitman's passionate voice so exemplifies the idea of celebration and gratitude I could never read more than a few of his lines without getting so excited I'd have to stand and walk around the room. It was this amplitude of voice that I used when writing my poem. It was my life and bearing that I was after, of course, but in using the largess of his personality I was granting myself permission to, in a sense, fly with his wings, to see my world through the magnanimity of his visionary prowess. And when addressing these Kalamazoo College students about Whitman's poem, I asked them to do what I did myself so many years later: to imagine feeling such immense spirit and generosity toward oneself and one's fellow men and women, toward all of creation; to imagine standing away from one's own belittlements and fears and stepping into the skin of such amplitude and well-being and addressing what one perceives as being most meager and damaged about oneself with his appetite for sympathy and kindness. I asked them to imagine believing in such appetite and then listening to their own longings and regrets in the voices of the unveiled past. And to my surprise, that's exactly what happened. In many cases, these young freshmen then became excited enough to try on Holden Caulfield's persona in Salinger's *Catcher in the Rye*, Huck Finn's "I" in *Adventures of Huckleberry Finn*, and Binx Bolling's in *The Moviegoer*, all strong, colorful narrators that, to some degree, helped them gain enough distance and perspective to establish an emotional connection with a reader. The ironic self-consciousness of Holden Caulfield's persona in particular allowed them to reevaluate their own material in a larger, more entertaining context; in imitating his voice their stories took on a greater emphasis, a wider reach and comic subtext. Suddenly, in taking on such vivid personalities their own autobiographical stories became charged with what we all saw as a borrowed excitement, as if suddenly they were sources of inspiration, opportunities for more inspired language and style, rather than entities unto themselves. Wasn't this the genius behind Salinger, Twain, and Percy's techniques: the voice of the narrator is its own important story, much more than a mere means of communicating information. Melville knew that Ishmael's voice had to be as dramatically compelling as Ahab's obsession with the white whale, or the story would never reach the level of drama and persuasion he desired; as Twain understood that Huck's voice had to compete with the great river itself, and all the larger-than-life characters he encountered while traveling it. In *The Moviegoer* Binx's voice was constructed to be as entertaining as New Orleans, Mardi Gras, and all the movies Binx found so inspiring. The autobiographical "I" of my students, I explained, was a loose stand-in for who they thought they might be at a given moment, and thus an amorphous and abstract notion instead of a carefully perceived presence, which didn't give their imaginations room to flourish.

I could now, in this private class, experiment more freely with these notions about fiction and fact and how they combine in a creative piece, and it didn't take long to realize that, as a result of the absence of a persona narrator, a similar equation existed in the early drafts of all these writers: their poems and stories were all 90 percent autobiographical and 10 percent imaginative. In other words, 90 percent mundane and predictable, and 10 percent invented and interesting. It became clear quickly that without a narrator most of what they wrote objectified factual and biographical information, which seldom feels true or alive, and in order to help them engage the reader's imagination and reverse this equation, I had to first find a way to help them engage their own.

I can give an example from an early version of one of my poems, "Greed." I didn't yet know what it was exactly that I was trying to say, only that I wanted to use my hometown of East Hampton during a recession as an example of what I saw as greed. Without knowing it, I was using an autobiographical "I" to just get the story down, or what I saw as the story. The results are a complete lack of a persona, and flat, lifeless language:

A man this morning
hailing a taxi, told his cell phone that
he was too busy to enjoy his new house in Nantucket.
"Everyone thinks, because I'm a banker, I think
Greed is good." Each day now in my ocean town,
waiting for work, more men stand staring into
the tedium of the sky over the railroad station.
Because it's thought the Hispanics will work
for less, they get chosen first. The whites and blacks
look dazed, as if they don't understand why
they're despised. My town depends on
real estate, tourism and construction.

Without a persona, I was using observation and information to make a point, as in an argument. This version was written on December 12, 2011. I began the poem the previous June, during the height of the Great Recession, and some sixty drafts later I finally found the correct persona, that of a sympathetic reporter, say, the kind Walker Percy might employ, who wants to state the facts of his story simply, but is also willing, if somewhat reluctantly, to give examples from his own life. Once I embodied and trusted this persona, the poem came quickly.

GREED

My ocean town struggles
to pick up leaves,
offer summer school,
and keep our library open.
Every day now
more men stand at the railroad station,

waiting to be chosen for work.
Because it's thought
the Hispanics will work for less
they get picked first,
while the whites and blacks
avoid each other's eyes.
Our handyman, Santos,
who expects only
what his hands earn,
is proud of his half acre in Guatemala,
where he plans to retire.
His desire to proceed with dignity
is admirable, but he knows
that now no one retires,
everyone works harder.
My father imagined a life
more satisfying than the one
he managed to lead.
He didn't see himself as uneducated,
thwarted, or bitter,
but soon-to-be rich.
Being rich was his right, he believed.
Happiness, I used to think,
was a necessary illusion.
Now I think it's just
precious moments of relief,
like dreams of Guatemala.

Of the many pleasures in teaching this class I especially enjoyed
the fact that I had both poets and fiction writers in the same class,
which I couldn't do in an academic setting. The fiction writers,

for instance, found it helpful to experiment with a poem's narrator to tell a more interior, intensely lyrical, and focused story, and the poets to use as a model a fictional narrator to relate a more expanded, linear, and narrative story. In criticizing one another's work, they learned new techniques they could then apply to their own work; fiction writers benefited from a more expressionistic and lyrical approach while poets could experience the advantages of narrative structure and empathizing with various characters, each enlarging his or her critical and technical vocabulary. And occasionally they would each realize their affinity for the other's form and an interesting, liberating swapping of identity would take place.

All of which led to my starting a craft class in which I would discuss the use of persona narrators in novels and poetry collections. Over time this class has evolved into a weekly event in which my other teachers and I, along with occasional invited guest writers and poets, discuss the various techniques used in works of fiction, poetry, and memoir, and the particular reasons each persona narrator was selected. Students would then turn these discussions into exercises to bring into their workshops. Eventually, the real purpose of the class became obvious: teaching people how to read as writers, which means examining the technical consequences of each individual decision a writer makes, the intention being to allow students to see every version and draft of their poems and stories as a step forward in an ongoing process of discovery rather than a scorecard of failure and discouragement. Young writers sometimes view their learning curves in mostly negative terms, as if experience and knowledge were a horse race with only winners and losers, and not the marathon of endurance it is. It's important to help beginning writers understand that making a successful poem or story is a process of trial and error, and that disappointment and confusion are important parts of the process.

Encouraging some students to apply the criticism they get in class to subsequent drafts of their work can prove difficult; writing several drafts of the same work can be intimidating and many prefer to apply criticism to only new work; though they all believe they want to publish their work, revision may seem too professional and therefore intimidating. Which is why when I first started teaching this private class, in order to stress the importance of making an emotional connection with the reader, I wouldn't let a student read more than a few paragraphs or even a beginning stanza if there wasn't a persona narrator.

When Jennifer Egan joined this class in the mid-Eighties, she frequently brought in disconnected work that didn't have a narrator. Her technical sophistication and narrative savvy were obvious from the beginning, but like most young writers of ambition she was in a great hurry to get on to the next scene, point, and story and when she didn't have a connected narrator, I wouldn't let her continue reading. "I think we've heard enough," is what she remembers my saying when I felt it was time for her to stop reading. Though obviously frustrating, it seemed the only way to get her to slow down long enough to understand the importance of making an emotional connection with the reader, of remembering and acknowledging the reader's presence. When she did get it, it happened quickly, and mostly through what she learned in criticizing the work of other students. In many cases, a writer's critical skills develop before their technical skill, which takes endless practice and patience. Most good writers learn first to be good critics, because it's easier to develop critical skills while giving criticism and not receiving it. Much of the learning that takes place occurs during the discussions when everyone is struggling to recognize and articulate what isn't working in someone else's work, everyone, that is, except the person whose work it is, who's too busy trying to understand the criticism to be able to hear even 10 to 15 percent of what's being said. Hearing good, constructive criticism isn't an inherited gift, it's something we must teach ourselves, such as using the fear of drowning to teach ourselves to swim. Which is why I don't let the writers talk during their critiques, because most of what they say is defensive, which often discourages further discussion and only makes it harder for them to hear something helpful. Learning to hear and then apply constructive criticism is one of the most difficult things for writers to learn, even accomplished writers. No one wants to hear that something they worked hard on doesn't work, but without constructive criticism it's often impossible to learn how to revise one's work. It's through our criticism of others' work that we learn how to revise our own; in fact, there's no better way of encouraging the development of a critical intelligence than by encouraging students to help others revise and strengthen their work.

The first time Jenny brought in pages with a connected narrator I wasn't sure who was most excited, she, I, or all the other students. As she remembers this, she burst into tears when I said "go on" with her reading of the story, as she was so accustomed to being asked to stop. I was then so disconcerted by what she later described as her "flood of tears that you rushed to get me wine to calm me down before I read the second half" of her story. I served wine then, maybe because William Dickey, a fine poet and teacher of mine at SF State College in the Sixties, did, also meeting classes in his home, and I remember nearly tripping over myself in my excitement to get her a glass. The look on her face—surprise mixed with relief and joy—was reward enough. Her few pages became her first published story.

It's probably impossible to ever really know the particular role I play in someone's writing life, but I do know that teaching is a genealogy of ardor and confidences, of the worries and regrets of things said and left unsaid that gets passed along from all my mentors to my students. I know exactly what compels in me so stringent an identification, makes me want to reveal whose voice it is they hear when their views of themselves turn dark and turbulent and they feel most hopeless and irrelevant. It's the same voice my father used while talking to himself in the bathroom each morning during his last months, washing in the bathroom sink, putting on the same clothes he wore the day before, gulping down his one cup of coffee and shred of toast before rushing out the door to suffer the ignominy of another bankrupt day; the voice that spoke to me when I couldn't learn to read or write, that told me to accept my place at the dummy table; the voice I taught myself to ignore when I first attempted to write by inventing a larger and more exciting voice that would argue against it by combining the voices of all the narrators in all the novels, poems, and stories I loved. It's the voice, when given a persona narrator, that must overcome all the comforts of the abyss.

The human capacity for self-delusion is one of our oldest fascinations, and privileges; in fact, our appetite for obliviousness, how little we understand the reasons we make life-changing decisions, our treasured sense of absolute bafflement and ineptitude, is often a more interesting story than the one we're trying to write. A serious work of imagination calls into question the important decisions we make and our reasons for making them. However prepossessing and entertaining the Hamlet story is—on its surface a story about avenging his father's murder, a willingness to sacrifice everything out of loyalty and obeisance to his father's memory and ghost—its real value is the preordained truth it reveals about how far some of us are willing to go to escape our true nature, the humiliation that we are willing to suffer in order to facilitate this evasion.

THE SOCRATIC METHOD

One of the reasons I borrowed our school's name from the Actors Studio was pretty mundane: there was no apostrophe after the word "Actors," indicating, to my mind at least, that they didn't want to imply ownership, the word "actor" was descriptive, not possessive, describing a community of striving artists plying their craft in a certain style and manner. And that's what I wanted, a collective of striving writers all pulling together, an industry of individual struggle and strength aimed at something communally distinctive. All I really knew about them was that they used a method devised by the Russian acting teacher Konstantin Stanislavsky, and that their director, Lee Strasberg, used his Socratic method of teaching, a form of teaching that asks focused and probing questions in a dialogue with students with the objective of inspiring critical thinking. Since my own method involved asking students the kind of small, specific questions I asked myself while writing and always wished my writing teachers had asked me, I found myself attracted to not only their name but what I understood to be Socrates's goal in asking his questions: self-knowledge and the wisdom derived from emotional truth. "The unexamined life is not worth living," I would quote him as saying at his trial for impiety, where, threatened with exile, which he saw as life without self-examination and therefore a fate worse than death, he, not unlike my friend Ralph Dickey, chose death.

If some of the questions I initially asked were perceived as being perhaps too personal and intrusive and if I sometimes got looks of agitated annoyance, it seemed a worthwhile risk. I would make it clear I wasn't prying but demonstrating the kind of self-examination all serious writers go through in determining what it is we're trying to say. And I soon discovered a good way of doing this was to ask others in the class what else they wished a writer would address in their work. When one writer, for instance, addressed only positive feelings in a poem about her relationship with her mother when the stress and upset was clear, I'd ask another student in the class if there was something else he or she wished had been revealed. "At least some anger or maybe resentment," one writer said. And when asked why and for what another student writer said, "For not being loved enough." I then asked the poet if she agreed the poem would be stronger if these emotions and their reasons were included. Yes, she said, indicating by her manner that she was aware of all this. My next question was obvious, though not the answer. I asked why she chose not to deal with her anger in the poem and she said, after barely a pause, "I didn't want to hurt anyone." The class seemed stunned silent. No one there, including myself, didn't fear the same thing. Revenge sometimes plays a part in our decisions, but only rarely; more often it's the very emotions that make us vengeful and that we most desire to express that render us silent. Judiciously placed questions can help writers realize not only their intentions but what exactly they fear most in revealing them.

One student insisted on writing stories about a highly competitive father character without ever going near the one emotion that was clear to every other student in the class: his rage. When I once asked him why he thought the father character found it necessary to humiliate and defeat every attempt his son made to succeed—didn't such an instinct go against the basic paternal desire to foster and encourage one's progeny?—the writer, surprising us all, blurted out that it was a despicable degree of juvenile envy and selfishness. The force with which he said this surprised him most of all. Never before had he been able to identify how he felt about his father's domination. Such questions can be unsettling, but also crucial in finding a story's true direction and meaning. The more interesting question, for instance, isn't why someone chooses to remain in an abusive relationship, but why the writer or character needs to tell their story, and at what personal cost. It's certainly an easier and more indirect, if not relaxed, way of going around the disabling emotion. The most powerful material is often the most subjective and disturbing, and therefore the most difficult to ascertain. It's helpful to point out that it's these same difficult emotions that we're trying to reveal in our characters, and ourselves, that readers most identify with and are moved by; it is what binds us and is the source of their gratitude and trust.

Another example is a student who struggled for a very long time to write about leaving her husband for another woman. She hadn't realized how unhappy she'd been in her marriage, or that she was capable of loving someone with such intensity, and the fact that it was another woman and not a man that ignited such passion seemed to matter most to others, her parents and friends, and especially her husband, who stopped speaking to her. Her children were suddenly part of a blended family with three other, very different children, and their struggle to accept this new life created additional confusion and suffering. Such a compelling story requires courage to write, which she has to spare, but her shame at having hurt her husband and children inhibited her ability to find a narrator who could summon the kind of sympathy that would allow her to realize the complexity of this story. After she persisted in her struggle, I asked a question that I knew entailed some risk. A thin line sometimes exists between asking something that may prove illuminating and asking something too volatile to abide, but the right question at a time when the writer can hear it can make all the difference.

I asked if her narrator should be held entirely responsible for whatever difficulties existed in her marriage, especially since in most marriages there's more than enough culpability to go around; and if not, whether her persona felt entitled to express what she really felt about her husband as a person and not just a man. Though she couldn't answer at the time, a few weeks later she brought in a Kafka exercise that brilliantly used his audacious and prosecutorial persona narrator in his *Letter to the Father* to address her father with all the rage and acuity that was missing from her previous poems about her husband. The object of her persona's anger didn't seem to matter; what she seemed to fear most was the force of her anger, and the hurt it might cause. Fear is a lottery only fear wins.

ANOTHER EXAMPLE OF THIS METHOD is the manner in which I found a narrator for the long poem at the heart of my book *Failure*, "The Wandering Wingless," which deals with the horrors of 9/11. The very idea of writing about this subject filled me with guilt and remorse and I couldn't even think about it without becoming depressed. The windows of my apartment on Charles Street were covered with the dust of human remains; the absence of the giant towers of the World Trade Center covered every street in the West Village like a giant shadow; one of my longtime students, Russ Siller, had lost his younger firefighter brother, Stephen Siller (in whose name the Tunnels to Towers run is made each year), and we had just given a benefit reading to raise money for his widow and five children; while another of my students had lost her husband, who worked in the North Tower, and was suddenly a widow with two small children. Feeling lost, I would walk the mile and a half to the rubble and stare into the surrounding gloom, holding in contempt my every reason and instinct to deal with such material—what right did I, who lost no one and was unharmed, have to deal with such devastation? In an attempt to resist my shitbird's willful logic, I reminded myself that I was a writer, a poet, and a citizen of the place where such devastation occurred and that dealing with difficult subjects was not only my right but my job; in fact, it's what I taught my students: that certain subjects choose us, not us them.

But nothing worked; stumped, I was ready to abandon it when I remembered my own technique and asked myself what it was in this subject that I so feared and couldn't tolerate even thinking about. Another trip to the rubble provided the answer: I was afraid I would remain stuck in what felt like a permanent state of suspension between anger and self-loathing, a state that reminded me of the seventy-two hours I'd spent in a psych ward in San Francisco when I was twenty and depressed after receiving a Dear John letter from the girl I loved. Penniless and without friends in a new place, I was enraged one moment and then overcome by shame for feeling this way the next. Unable to tolerate such self-loathing, oblivion seemed the only comfort until a doctor at the ward, having learned what I studied in school, asked what I imagined a reader might find interesting if this experience was turned into a story. I said how hard it was to trust anyone, especially those we loved. Even thinking about writing about what I was suffering helped enormously; the one thing I knew I could trust was my writing, which provided a very good reason to live.

I no sooner began taking notes about these memories than these lines came, which inspired me to begin my long poem:

                      The night
tasted of lilac and spring.
Beyond Golden Gate Park
I could hear ocean waves.
My hands were shaking.
What was I doing here,
in this public pain?
Everything I loved I feared.
Was this what failure was—
endless fear? My face
pressed against cold bars,
every muscle
in the universe relaxed
as piss flowed warm
and free down
both my legs
all the way to hell.

The sense of vicarious trauma that exists between writers and guilt-inducing subject matter creates a feeling of marginalization and lack of privilege. What I needed, I decided, was a perspective so preoccupied and detached it would let me view my subject sideways, at an angle sufficient to the objectivity I needed. Having brought my own two dogs to the Washington Square Park dog run before and after the event and seen the degree to which everyone there sought refuge in their dogs in times of tragedy, I made my nameless first-person narrator a dog walker too fearful of intimacy to own one himself. I then used the existential sweetness of Walker Percy's narrator Binx Bolling as a model, which provided the distance and perspective that my new persona narrator needed to tell the larger, more historic story of national catastrophe. And having read how the psych ward at St. Vincent's Hospital had to be emptied to make room for the expected injured (there were few) and since everyone I knew now existed in a state of shock, I placed my narrator on the street on the day of the event, after having just suffered electroshock treatment and been evacuated from the hospital. This nameless narrator knew not only what the story was but how to tell it. As Ronald Gregor Smith points out in his preface to Martin Buber's *I and Thou*, teaching takes place in dialogues between the personal and the impersonal, the world to be "used" and the world to be "met." For writers it's a dialogue between our relationship with our feelings and the mystery of our experience, between what happened to us and our struggle to make sense of it.

The shitbird's sole agenda is to negate and revoke; it uses confusion to disseminate remorse and self-reproach; its favorite phrases are "I don't know," "I have no right," and "I don't want to hurt anyone." The single most difficult thing in teaching writing is selecting, simplifying, and adjusting our comments to what someone at his or her particular stage of development can hear at that moment and asking the right question at the right time, especially if that someone is ourselves, while the single most difficult thing in writing is daring to look at what most wants to stay invisible and impermeable. The questions we ask ourselves as writers open not only our minds but our hearts and souls. If we can dare to go *there*, to pursue what most frightens us, whatever wisdom and insight we may find will most certainly be of equal value to our readers, who also appreciate the difficulties involved in pursuing the truth.

IN THE NATURE OF A TEST

I was twenty-six and teaching at Kalamazoo College when I first read Joan Didion's *Play It as It Lays*. Feeling my professional life as a teacher and writer had finally begun, I returned from giving a poetry reading in a nearby town and found that Marie had moved out, leaving a note on her side of our bed that said she needed "a little time to myself." This wasn't the first time Marie had done this and after a few days I began to believe what my shitbird was telling me: that I was being punished for believing I'd finally amounted to something. The Yiddish word for this is *kenahora*, meaning, "may no evil eye befall you," which is an ancient Jewish belief that in allowing ourselves to feel successful we call forth the very thing we fear most: our doom. If anyone ever said anything even remotely positive in my grandma's presence she would spit twice over her left shoulder and run around the house tying red ribbons to anything that looked menacing, like doorknobs and chairs. In a sense, the shitbird serves the same purpose. Good fortune is only an illusion; all my hard work in getting two degrees, publishing a few poems and stories, and now this new teaching job, only appeared to represent good fortune. Not wanting anyone in the faculty to know, I moved off-campus in the dead of night, to a small apartment in town, where I could suffer without interference. Teaching became a drudgery—who was I to think I had anything to offer students; I hadn't written anything of value and didn't have a PhD so I wasn't really qualified to teach literature. The fact that I'd been hired over many other applicants and had won the affectionate respect of my students and a few colleagues—well, as I now saw things, I'd obviously conned my way into this job the same way I'd tricked my graduate program into believing I was a genuine, promising writer; I should've known that whenever I was the least bit happy fate would find a way to disrupt things. It was obvious that I shouldn't have taken the job in the first place or brought my girlfriend along. (And no, I didn't recognize the origin of such perverse logic; the shitbird was an idea only Ralph suffered.)

It was in this mood that I found my way to reading Didion's novel *Play It as It Lays*, immediately becoming captivated by the fierceness of her narrator's honesty and confidence. Its vision was darker, harsher, more realistic and intelligent than anything I'd ever read before. Having no idea how to proceed myself, it was exactly the book I needed to read. I read it straight through over a weekend, marveling at the prescience of her third-person narrator that seemed more intimate than most writers' use of first. Though the desert world of gambling and moviemaking couldn't have been more alien to me, I felt as if I were reading my own story, written by someone who knew me better than I knew myself. I'd never read anything that so brazenly, bluntly, questioned the value of human life. In fact, that was its subject: the toll suffering took on those for whom suffering seemed to be a natural consequence of their way of life, a means in itself of determining their fate. I felt as if I were being asked to weigh the degree of light and dark that I carried around inside me, my reasons for wanting to continue to live. "Why are you here?" Maria asks BZ, knowing the answer. He replies, "Because you and I *know* something. Because we've been out there where nothing is. Because I wanted—you know why." He was about to kill himself, to deliberately overdose on Seconal, and she does nothing to stop him. He was choosing death because he didn't "have enough left to break a bottle over" as someone outside their motel room engaged in a bar fight apparently still did.

Late one night, in a fever of enthusiastic desperation, I wrote Didion a letter, just a few sentences about how much her book meant to me, and then ran down to a corner mailbox to post it before I could change my mind. I even managed to forget about it until, a week later, I received a reply. Never before had I so delicately, tentatively opened a letter.

It was a brief note thanking me for writing her, mentioning that she sensed from my letter that I too was a writer and was going through a difficult time. If possible, she suggested, I should try to see whatever I was going through in the nature of a test.

In the nature of a test!

How in the world did she know I was a writer, I'd avoided mentioning it, and even more baffling was the fact she'd somehow deduced that I was going through a dark time, I certainly hadn't mentioned it. And what did she mean by asking me to see my situation in the nature of a test—was she suggesting that I see my situation the way a writer would see a character's, the way she viewed Maria in first person and third person simultaneously, holding her close and at a sober distance, the way a philatelist might examine a curious stamp in order to determine its vintage and value? Was this how she managed to imagine so much about her characters and had guessed my state of mind from the little I wrote her? Was she, in sharing her gifts of perception and empathy, asking me to see myself as someone not pathetically hapless but in pain, to view myself as deserving of as much tolerant indulgence as a character in a novel; that I should give myself the benefit of the doubt, a gift I'd perhaps be generous enough to give most strangers?

Was she offering me the gift of perception, the gift of sympathy?

The idea was exciting, revelatory; this was the very thing Viktor Frankl wrote about in his book about surviving Auschwitz, *Man's Search for Meaning*, the very thing I wasn't able to help my friend Ralph Dickey see: that by placing one's predicament in a larger context one may be able to discover whatever meaning lies hidden there, meaning that might help us prevail. Maria was viewing BZ the way she viewed herself, without affectation, subterfuge, or self-pity, which gave her the strength and objectivity to see him as independent of their friendship and her feelings toward him. This permitted her to allow him to decide his own fate. This was in 1971, a year before Ralph Dickey killed himself, and for the first time I began to see him more objectively, as a story separate from mine, as deserving of his own self-image-and-judgments—who was I to demand he conform to my sense of him, to hold him accountable to my ambitions for him? After losing everything else, he still owned his own volition, his right to do with his story as he pleased. I then began to see Marie and me as characters desperate for acknowledgment and succor, fellow travelers on the same random journey, ultimately responsible for only our own actions. Maybe it wasn't anyone's fault, or even a matter of bad luck and fate, maybe we just didn't belong together, and leaving me was the only way she knew how to tell me. I was beginning to see things other than as a matter of blame and evil eyes, but as a test of personal accountability and reckoning, a test of self-worth and survival.

This changed how I saw everything. Within days I began a poem that more accurately addressed what I was feeling beneath the fog of self-loathing and blame, which was a profound sense of sadness and loss. I began to understand how in our own peculiar ways we'd helped each other survive many hard times, how she'd stayed with me when I most needed her, through graduate school and starting a new life as a teacher and professional writer. I was stronger now and maybe she just knew it was time to begin her life anew. It was enough that we'd somehow managed to love each other as best we could. I reread the end of a letter she'd sent to me some weeks after she left: "I want you to know really know what the past three years have meant to me emotionally. I want you to not be hurt that . . . I can't see you right now. I want to get myself so you can see who I am and love me for that. I love you and don't want you to be hurt by what I need for myself. Please be happy with yourself. I love you and want everything for you."

I'd read this without taking any of it in, feeling it, all I could understand was that she was leaving me, again, but now I was seeing her and our situation through Maria's eyes and this was the perspective, the mood and tone, the persona I wanted in my poem. I then began what turned out to be my most successful poem, which five years later appeared in the *New Yorker* and became the title poem of my first book of poems, *Like Wings*.

LIKE WINGS

Last night I dreamed I was the first man to love a woman
& woke shaking & went out to watch
the faded rag of the sky burn into dawn.
I am tired of the river before feeling,
the joy we must carve from shadow,
tired of my road-thick tongue.

I cannot hand you my breath or wrap the horizon
around your wrist & be forgiven,
I cannot rub the dry wood of my ribs to fire

& sleep. The edge of sleep isn't sleep.
I go room to room tying my feelings into knots.
The space we filled now fills me.
The light & dark won't mix.

I cannot leave myself like a house frozen in the background.
I am this body and the weather all year round.
I think of the light that opened over you our first morning,
how the glass in my lungs turned to sound
& I saw you woman & child & couldn't breathe, for love.
Fear is the edge that is the risk that is loving.
It stinks of blood, draws sharks.

The nights you waltzed naked round our bed,
myself holding the chair I'd painted blue again,
the cats flowing in the wings of your good yellow hair.
There is much men don't know about women,
how your hands work the air to water, the seed to life,
why the salt at the tips of your breasts glows
& tastes of mollusk.

There are hours when the future gives up all hope
& stops in the middle of busy streets
& doesn't care. But think of the distance we have come,
the hands which have wound us.
There will be others.

I have read of ancient people
who held razors to their doctor's throat
as he operated—as if love could have such balance,
like wings.

One night I followed your tracks through deep snow
& stood in an old schoolhouse watching the new sun
come red & shimmer over the opening fields,
the world white & flat & a light
I'd known all my life burned in my head like a fist of rags,
how I couldn't remember what we feared
we'd taken or left,
my arms opened to your shape, how I couldn't lift
out of my body, my mouth frozen
round the sound of your name.

This new way of looking at things through the prism of another writer's narrator provided the kind of freedom Cioran had spoken of; by adapting and turning despair against itself and, in a sense, using it as inspiration and even comfort. I soon began asking my students to do exactly what I was now asking myself to do: turn a difficult time in their lives into a scene being played out on a stage, and to imagine actors standing in for themselves, and then describe the action through the eyes of someone sitting in the front row, a director or member of the audience, who was viewing the drama from the more objective distance of a dark auditorium. And for this new narrator they should find a voice they trusted, an older brother or sister, a friend, or a narrator from a book they loved, that would enable them to see this time with a greater degree of curiosity and sympathy. I was surprised and delighted with the results I got from these freshman students, which helped the fiction writers and poets alike connect to a new and more profound level of feeling. It was the first truly successful assignment I'd given them, the first time I felt like a teacher. Until now I'd seen these young men and women as floundering and perhaps even ungifted, but now I saw that it was I who had been floundering, as a teacher and a writer. Without knowing it, I'd been asking them to do something that was extremely hard and entirely new to them, without providing them with a clear description of the task or the necessary tools. All writers write for the same reasons—to turn experience into meaning and meaning into verification. Spinoza tells us in his *Ethics* that our suffering will end once we can turn it into an image we can see, and as Walker Percy so powerfully demonstrates in *The Moviegoer*, people love seeing their house or street in movies because only then do those things, and they themselves, seem real and alive. We seek the solace of verification, the ardor found in the particular visual reality of our existence.

YEARS LATER, WHILE LIVING IN New York City and teaching at NYU, I met Joan Didion at a party given in a lavish Park Avenue apartment by one of the sponsors of a PEN International writers' conference. She was sitting off by herself in a library, away from the large gathering down the hall, and she looked so private and content I almost didn't recognize her. But it was her all right, there was no mistaking her from her photos, that quality of "fierce fragility," the phrase she'd used to so accurately describe Maria. She looked up and smiled and I went over and introduced myself, reminding her of the note she'd written me more than ten years before, and of the letters we'd exchanged since. Smiling warmly, she motioned for me to sit next to her on the sofa. She not only remembered my letter, she said, she enjoyed reading my poems in various places and was happy to know I was doing well. We immediately began speaking like old acquaintances, discussing the other writers we knew at the party, and the New York literary life. Surprised at how easy speaking to her was, I found the courage to ask the one thing I'd been curious about ever since I first received her letter: how she had surmised from my few words that I was a writer.

"How did you know I was a writer, or wanted to be? I thought I did such a good job of not mentioning it."

"You were so attuned to style and language, you just sounded like one. Who else would care so much?"

I then mentioned her advice that I should see whatever I was going through in the nature of a test. It had helped me get through a number of dark times, I said, and I had even managed to turn the idea into a philosophy of writing I taught to this day.

She just smiled, somewhat curiously.

What seemed so perspicacious then still amazes me: our need for a fair-minded and independent arbiter, one more inclined to truth than the mercy we may seek; in fact, one who shows as little mercy to her characters as they deserve, mercy not being the point, however unbearably exquisite it might be.

THE MAP OF THE WORLD

*Sometimes I imagine the map of the world spread out
and you stretched diagonally across it. And I feel as if
I could consider living in only those regions that either
are not covered by you or are not within your reach.
And in keeping with the conception I have of your
magnitude, these are not many and . . . marriage is not
among them.*

—FRANZ KAFKA, *LETTER TO THE FATHER*

Kafka wrote this letter near the end of his young life, after
he'd written his major works, so he perhaps saw it as a last
act of, what—remorse, resolution, revenge? Stating his case
as man and son, he was reestablishing his boundaries and rights of
selfhood the way a lawyer, which he was, might, so his father would
know how he perceived their relationship, and how he had been
affected by it. Certainly, whatever reasons he owned for writing it,
its inevitability as a statement of cause and effect reveals a logic or
argument he may not have himself fully understood, an argument,
say, as compulsive as it is hypnotic. I don't believe it's too much to
claim that all or much of his work comes out of the disorder and
turbulence (not to mention guilt, shame, and genius) that produced
this argument, which then evolved into an obsession with collecting

evidence of injustice and transgression that inspired one of the most influential visions in literary history.

I've used this quote from his letter many times in classes, often to illustrate how a metaphor or image can state what might otherwise feel or actually be inexpressible, and each time I used it I'd consider teaching the book in our craft class and then quickly would find a reason not to, without bothering, or wanting, to understand why. Whatever fascinated me in these few words obviously also terrified me, something larger, more prescient and disturbing than I cared to realize.

A year ago, after reading the new translation of *Letter to the Father* by Ernst Kaiser and Eithne Wilkins, I decided to teach the book, not because the differences from other translations were in any way dramatic, but because I could now see, with the perspective of time, that Kafka's goal wasn't simply to repair or perhaps rectify what he perceived as being unjust and inequitable in his relationship with his father, it was something much more ardent and perhaps overpowering: an attempt to examine the very nature of his own being as he saw it reflected in the man who played the role of his father. I say "played the role" because this letter was clearly designed as a book, a work of imagination, not unlike his novels and stories in which all the characters have designated roles. It was more personal and historical than his other books, a "letter" addressed to only one person, which makes it all the more universal and intimate for its portrayal of family dystopia and cruelty, because his persona was clearly aware that with each accusation, he was presenting his case to an audience larger than one man. The fact that he gave the finished letter to his mother to give to his father (which she never did, not even after Kafka died, wanting to protect both parties, and which he may have anticipated) and understood that his friend, future biographer, and literary executor, Max Brod, would see and no doubt eventually publish it, meant that on some level he wanted it to be known. And I'm not using the word "case" lightly, because it seems clear that this rather dramatic reinvention of tribal conflict was being cast as a trial in which his father was the defendant, his persona the prosecuting attorney, and, most important, he himself, the child and man, the plaintiff.

Yes, the author of one of the most original works of the twentieth century, *The Trial*, was now staging another trial, this time casting his persona as a prosecutor instead of a defendant or victim. If his use of a map as a symbol of suppression and victimhood was impressive, the new metaphor he was now using was even more original, and disturbing; in recasting the central turmoil of his childhood and wretched adolescence as a trial, he was in effect placing his father on the witness stand, without the will or recourse to speak and defend himself. His father's silence is by itself a verdict of guilt that Kafka must've found profoundly gratifying. The personage who dominates the very map of the world is slyly rendered mute and, in a sense, defenseless. Who among us would not enjoy, if we had the imagination and resolve, the satisfaction of placing our most pronounced antagonist on trial, without the luxury or freedom to speak in his or her defense?

Indeed, what a wonderful exercise this would make for my students, who would all own an argument against someone they would benefit from identifying. Kafka's father, or the argument he turned him into, was most certainly his black bird, an internal barometer of self-worth, perhaps the very fascination that drew me to this metaphor—didn't we all live in one kind of argument or another, endlessly seeking to appease or avenge whatever injustice we couldn't bring ourselves to forgive? Didn't we all desire retribution, some kind of public shaming, and then suffer the resulting guilt and shame? Isn't this why I so feared teaching Kafka's book, and turning it into an exercise?

Even if my students failed to identify or articulate their arguments, the very idea of such a confrontation might inspire in them greater courage and forbearance, which, given the shitbird's love of disguises and invisibility, was half the battle. And if a student could go no further than imagining his or her antagonist, the recipient of their letter, they would encounter, in a more prescribed and explicit way, as Kafka himself did, their most ascendant personas.

My students immediately took to the exercise in a way I hadn't imagined. One wrote to an alcoholic father, another to an abusive husband, and another to a mother who disapproved of everything she desired and dreamed of pursuing. The letterform-imposed structure and compression, and the idea of using Kafka's prosecutorial persona, spared them some real portion of shame; it provided a powerful mask to hide behind and many seemed to delight in their newfound prosecutorial powers, demonstrating little mercy on their defendants. One student in particular confronted a father whose drunken rages so intimidated her as a child she could never before even realize how much she desired to express the dormant anger that suppressed her every creative impulse. And, ironically, the required legal nomenclature and diction came naturally to her, coming as she did from a family of lawyers. Her plaintiff was her innocence and individuality, and each of us in class, stupefied by her strength and courage, became not only a member of a carefully selected jury but a witness to a performance so persuasive no one, not one of us, could say anything after she stopped reading. It was an exercise in selfhood unlike any other any of us had heard, one perfectly suited to both Kafka's and her own candor.

———

AND THEN I OF COURSE tried to imagine writing one myself. But I'd written about my father many times before in poems and stories, and I wasn't sure what would be gained in my prosecuting him once again. Kafka and many of these students were addressing people still very much alive, with whom there still existed an active relationship and the hope of at least a limited reconciliation, while my father had been dead for well over fifty years. As Kafka tells his father: "You can only treat a child the way you yourself are constituted, with vigor, noise, and hot temper . . . because you wanted to bring me up to be a strong brave boy." A letter of such perspicacity and judgment would require great strength of vision and willfulness, but he most certainly hadn't become the strong brave boy his father desired in any conventional sense. He goes on to say: "I was a timid child . . . obstinate. . . . Mother spoilt me too, but I cannot believe that a kindly word . . . friendly look, could not have got me to do anything that was wanted of me." Yes, but what did he imagine was wanted of him, what degree of meekness and compliance— the kind that would turn him into a Joseph K, a prey who could be arrested without reason, the kind of mole-like being and insect he wrote about in "The Burrow" and "The Metamorphosis," creatures so undesirable they must live in isolation, away from all human contact? If this is what he imagines his father wanted him to be, then a letter like this is all the more crucial and piquant, all the more existential.

In revealing his defendant's character to the jury, and to us, his future readers, Kafka isn't merely pleading with his father to see and love him for who he is and was, any more than a prosecutor would plead with a defendant for understanding; the charge he is making is that of willful abuse and neglect, of disdain and indifference, and in the very act of prosecution he is liberating his adolescent self from having to see himself through his father's eyes.

I now see that I was doing a similar thing in this poem from my book *Failure*:

THE ONE TRUTH

After dreaming of radiant thrones
for sixty years, praying to a god
he never loved for strength, for mercy,
after cocking his thumbs
in the pockets of his immigrant schemes,
while he parked cars during the day
and drove a taxi all night,
after one baby was born dead,
and he carved the living one's name
in windshield snow in the blizzard of 1945,
after scrubbing piss, blood
and vomit off factory floors
from midnight to dawn,
then filling trays with peanuts,
candy and cigarettes
in his vending machines all day,
his breath a wheezing suck
and bellowing gasp
in the fist of his chest,
after washing his face, armpits
and balls in cold back rooms,
hurrying between his hunger
for glory and his fear
of leaving nothing but debt,
after having a stroke and
falling down factory stairs,

his son screaming at him
to stop working and rest,
after being knocked down
by a blow he expected all his life,
his son begging forgiveness,
his wife crying his name,
after looking up at them
straight from hell, his soul
withering in his arms—
is this what failure is,
to end where he began,
no one but a deaf dumb God
to welcome him back,
his fists pounding at the gate—
is this the one truth,
to lie in a black pit
at the bottom of himself,
without enough breath
to say goodbye
or ask for forgiveness?

My father died bankrupt and defeated, a fate he appeared to call upon himself. If Kafka's father's shadow covered the world, my father's shadow created a legacy of failure, anger, and shame. This third-person persona allowed me to address the nature of my grief and to indict my father on charges of vainglory and willful blindness, while distributing blame between him and myself in equal measure, with some suggestion of sympathy and regret, if not forgiveness. My defendant was also the plaintiff, the eighteen-year-old boy who witnessed the heartbreak of his father's self-destruction. If I were to write such a letter, I wouldn't ask my younger self to understand or forgive his father, who viewed him as an unsolicited responsibility and annoyance, but to understand and forgive himself, to see himself in the nature of a test, as a person of imagination and goodwill, deserving of the respect and affection his father was incapable of providing. I would plead with him to put into perspective his father's inadequacies as an immigrant who came to this country as a boy of six speaking not a word of English and who, without the benefit of education or guidance, would have to make his way while helping four younger brothers and two sisters; that he see himself as the only child of a great appetite for acknowledgment and restitution.

I would ask him to imagine himself as the man, poet, husband, and father he would become, to view himself through the prism of this more gracious and generous regard.

I would speak to him not as an ungrateful reprobate unworthy of his father's strength of will, but as an innocent unfairly burdened with a legacy he would be made to tolerate and sustain for the rest of his life.

I would ask him what I ask of myself and of my students: to delight in qualities he alone possesses, to take pleasure in his own strengths, in the forlorn, frightened, doubting responsibility of his gladness; to define himself only by those qualities of temperament and sensitivity he himself made.

I would ask him to address his own magnitude, which his father could not.

GUSSIE

C reative writing is an act of great presumption and, in a sense, an act of ventriloquism and hubris. In order to find a narrator who will help us discover the secrets and meanings we're after, we must first struggle to find the suppleness, twist of intuition, and sober insight without which it's impossible to presume to know how to do or become anything, let alone a writer. The transformation we're after almost always involves our changing from someone we think or hope or fear we are and perhaps never were, to someone we want to be in our work, a change that involves risk and utter confusion, because we initially seldom understand what we're asking of ourselves, or one another. Which is to change in ourselves the utter predictability of our self-ignorance and, in a sense, to subject ourselves to the vows and prejudices of our illusions, regardless of the risks involved. We're asking ourselves to somehow become more clairvoyant, curious, and sympathetic, to merge our visions and ambitions into something new and oddly different, mixing the unrealized and incomplete with the witnessed and tolerated. In other words, we're asking ourselves to completely reinvent ourselves, to become new and authentic, and therefore deserving of our own illusions.

In a sense, many people fancy themselves original and artistic. Our mailman explains why dogs bark at him: "You come, they bark, you go away. They're control freaks." Our plumber delineates his rich and famous clients: "To the Jews I say I'm Puerto Rican, to the Christians, Jewish, to the famous, crazy, to the filthy rich, creative because above all else everyone wants to be richer, more famous, and crazier." My barber twirls his scissors, winks at my persona imprisoned in his mirrored infinity, and describes how the wrist, fingers, and scissors merge with the peculiar foliage of the beloved under the stress of relentless vanity and quest for perfection. How he becomes one with his client and understands their every wish.

One writer I worked with wrote stories about characters that all hated their old Westchester houses and country club privileges, the brutal expense and indomitable grief of their Irish Catholic immigrant heritage. One was molested by priests, and terrified of what in her remained unmolested. Other characters volunteered in soup kitchens and used-furniture shops, languishing among the volatile emergencies of the stricken and the discarded, which, like themselves, constantly apologized for sins of which they were not guilty. Married to a rich and dominating doctor, she found herself living in a world divorced from the one she was brought up in, an immigrant working-class world in which everyone knew and valued their heritage, having worked hard to transcend it. The wealth she married into felt to her unearned and hollow. She wanted her writing, I believed, to help her rid herself of the inept factory of her pummeled-into-oblivion self-esteem, to help her achieve some sense of tranquility and self-acceptance. Thus Gussie, a character that obeyed no laws other than spontaneity, curiosity, and freedom of will, sprang out of the cranky, bruised, autobiographical facts of her life, and blossomed first into a persona of pure fancy and desire, and then into a character who could do and say all the things she herself was afraid to, including defying a husband of whom she herself remained terrified.

Even an unreliable narrator must, within the confines of her own fictional realm, be or become, to herself at least, an authority. She was raised in a world where women were authorities only to their children, a world where self-cruelty and the tiny, unpardonable, ceaseless blasphemies and lamentations of one's real biography had to be repressed. This was the same world I grew up in. My mother, though a brilliant student, had to leave school in the tenth grade to help support her family. Her father, an Orthodox Jew, believed educating women deprived them of their true nature: to serve first God and then men. Despite the fact that two of her teachers and an esteemed guidance counselor came to her home to argue with her father on her behalf, she left school at fifteen to help support her family. Her deprivation became my salvation; she stressed education above all else; she stressed me above all else.

Books gave this writer permission to question her complete lack of trust in her own judgment. Of the many stories she started and couldn't finish, the one that most obsessed her dealt with her molestation by a priest when she was nine. In each version of this story the child's fear of the priest's authority—God's authority presumably—stopped her. How could she protest the actions of someone she and everyone in her community admired and looked up to; who would believe her over him? When she reached the point in the story where such a confrontation was necessary, she'd stop writing and turn to another story and subject entirely different, and safer. It wasn't until she found Gussie, or Gussie found her, that she was able to return to this subject, though now it was her husband's authority she was confronting.

At first she wanted a character who wouldn't be afraid to shut her study door when she wrote or give her home number to her therapist so her husband wouldn't know she was in therapy and assume he was the very subject he'd forbidden her to talk about;

a character who didn't have to hide her diary and cell phone in a safe-deposit box and would never leave her children and flee down a nighttime highway to get away from everything that reminded her of herself. A character, in other words, who wouldn't be ashamed of her, whom she'd want as a friend. Together, we understood that the fearless character she was seeking was actually a persona narrator who would help her overcome her fears. She looked at narrators in Alice Munro, Grace Paley, Ann Beattie, and Lydia Davis, one of Chekhov's, and even Nabokov's narrator (the gender of these narrators could be easily enough changed and adapted to one's subject and needs) in *Pale Fire*, all of whom seemed so preoccupied with so many prolix issues it might keep her focus off what most frightened her. She could inhabit none of them. They all remained silent or disappeared completely when her husband's character entered the story. She herself could be funny, bitterly, whimsically ironic, but none of the material she wrote about was, and none of these narrators seemed capable or willing to speak up for her. Then she met Clarissa Dalloway, and everything changed. Virginia Woolf's *Mrs. Dalloway* was a blend of Woolf's wonderfully revelatory third-person narrator and her character, Clarissa, and almost immediately she absorbed both the character and narrator into her bloodstream, read and reread the book over weeks, and months. Woolf's blissful joy in revealing everything going on in Clarissa's mind during this one day of preparing for a party allowed her to confront feelings she'd until now dutifully avoided. She quoted a passage she found especially inspiring: "But Proportion has a sister, less smiling, more formidable, a Goddess even now engaged—in the heat and sands of India, the mud and swamp of Africa, the purlieus of London, wherever in short the climate or the devil tempts men to fall from the true belief which is her own—is even now engaged in dashing down shrines, smashing idols, and setting up in their place her own stern countenance. Conversion is her name and she feasts on the wills of the weakly, loving to impress, to impose, adoring her own features stamped on the face of the populace."

Yes, Proportion now had a sister. In Woolf's novel the great flood of images and thoughts and colors pours forth on a river of sheer feminine confidence and authority—Woolf is in love with her prowess, is fully aware of the masterpiece of style and vision she's composing word by word, instinct by intuition, sinew by sinew, and all this was being absorbed into every facet of my student's consciousness and being. She would dream, she told me, of Woolf's use of interior monologue and then imitate her voice while driving to class. "Imagine Woolf saying, actually saying this out loud: 'How can one weigh and shape dialogue till each sentence tears the shingles in the bottom of the reader's soul?'—imagine that, please!"

Gussie was born out of her mastering and celebration of what she saw as heroic feeling, a shrine to the creative powers of persuasion and influence. She especially found enthralling Woolf's subtle use of uncertainty and incongruity—especially as it applied to Woolf's frank admission of aloneness, the solitude necessary to creative and spiritual realization—which provided her with the strength to embrace the thing she feared most, the very centerpiece of her victimhood: her helplessness.

It didn't seem all that long before Gussie wasn't satisfied in taking over her every scene of every story she wrote, but also began disrupting much of her life. Things she might not have even imagined thinking, let alone saying, she now said with confidence, such as the note she sent me after she met my soon-to-be wife at a school reading: "Marry her, immediately!" And when I found the courage and money to make a down payment on a wreck of a house in East Hampton during a recession, she sent me a boom box to entertain myself with while I and a legion of friends and hired help made my new house livable. At my fiftieth birthday party, she read a note toasting my chewed fingernails, misbuttoned shirts, and manner of stuttering in class when excited about any idea, good or bad, all now, as far as she was concerned, represented as precursors to my meeting my wife, Monica. And once, when she worried that a character as strong as Gussie required a much stronger and more self-assured writer, her certainty of absolute failure was so convincing that after our conversation ended, I found myself regretting everything I'd ever said to her, said to anyone, regretting not knowing how to answer, assuage, remove her pain. Should I have admitted that no one ever saves anyone, that teaching at best points a way in the dark, but nothing more; confessed that I sometimes didn't sleep the night before one of our sessions, described in my own therapy sessions her situation, fearing I'd say the wrong thing and somehow harm her further? What was I doing taking on such responsibility, I wasn't trained or qualified, I prided myself on never promising anyone anything, especially something as ethereal and complex as the rescue creative writing represented—had I learned nothing from my friendship with Ralph Dickey?

But then Gussie, the very sibilance of her name, seemed to change everything. "Guess what Gussie said to his face, yet!" she'd proclaim about this smart, fast-talking narrator that gave no quarter, who would, she believed, show her the way out of her unhappiness, and set her free. Wasn't this how I too had survived? she once asked me. She, who lived in a fancy suburban house and took golf trips around the world, was asking me, who made just enough to get by, to do for her what I'd done for myself, to, in some fashion, save her. Yes, she laughed after I asked if that was what she wanted, to in any way be like me, bitten nails and stuttering improbability and all? Yes, she said, because I lived according to my beliefs, while she denied hers.

When she heard about the birth of my first son, Eli, she called to say that now I had a subject worthy of my talents. "Do you know what I mean? It's important that you know."

I confessed that I wasn't sure.

"I mean now you have a family and can be the father you never had. Do you understand how important that is?"

I said I did but was too emotional to say anything more.

Sometimes I didn't know who was teaching whom, or what. Her goodness and generosity came from somewhere unique and private, I would tell her; her love of literature and determination were qualities that derived only from her. Sometimes I didn't know who I was talking to, her or me. Had I said this or had she, or maybe Gussie herself? I say so many things, attempting with technique and encouragement to move a writer one step closer to recognizing that there were at least two of them, one who admitted and understood nothing, who refused under any circumstance to acknowledge or use the knowledge we knew they possessed, and the one who admitted it freely, proudly, who recognized when her black bird was speaking and why. The open writer and the hidden one, both listening and nodding their heads and smiling at what was being said, explained, emphasized, and reiterated countless times, the one famished for instruction, movement, and success, and the one that rejected everything that held any scent of revelation. The one who connected to what was learned and the one who buried it immediately, decisively.

She was going further and faster than ever before, right up to the most difficult part of her story, when Gussie's husband screamed at her, breaking a chair against the wall behind her, threatening to destroy her reputation and take her children away if she left him. This is when she, holding her baby, smelled in the delectable texture of her hair her own innocence and strength, and found there the dignity of autonomy and rage, there, in the wellspring of her character's imagination, the strength and largess of her precious well-being:

> *Gussie dropped her head onto the baby's and brushed her lips against the soft hair.*
> *She allowed herself the luxury of a few caved-in moments, trying to find the strength to enter the house.*

She, who spent her life regretting just about everything, except for her children, was doing what she'd always wanted to do, what she'd always hoped her writing would permit her to do: to finally speak up on her own behalf, to represent herself as someone worthy of attention and sympathy.

Her illness came quickly, and irreversibly. We didn't speak for weeks, maybe a month. I knew only that she had to cancel several sessions. Then, sick with cancer, she called me from a hospital bed, her voice buoyant, telling me the not-yet-written end of her story: Gussie calls her mother from a highway to say she was headed north with her children, toward Canada, beginning all over again. She was only a few pages away from finishing it, she said, her children were all healthy and settled, everything was okay, finally, she just wished she had a little more time to finish her story and say goodbye to Gussie. Gussie was alive even if her story wasn't finished, even if no one besides her and me ever read it. She was alive and independent, she laughed, a character born of her imagination living the life she was afraid to, out there somewhere, heading north.

I CAME, I SAW, I SUFFERED

In an attempt to refine and order the disheveled past into something that might make us feel a little more presentable and necessary, we sometimes reconfigure our stories into lessons, warnings, or examples of how righteous or innocent or wronged we were, as if the meaning we seek doesn't actually exist, and they, our stories, can sometimes feel like overworked, befuddled, and unoriginal creatures, or beasts of burden, that are irrelevant as object lessons to others. One of my first writing teachers, the novelist Wright Morris, liked to entertain his classes by rephrasing the Latin phrase veni, vidi, vici (I came, I saw, I conquered) that Julius Cesar used to claim a quick victory in 47 BC, as: I came, I saw, I suffered. On one hand he was being ironic, signifying the "tales of woe" his young writing students so often portrayed their lives as being, and on the other, dead serious. The danger, he believed, in demonstrating excessive reverence for irreverent subjects, was to be caught exaggerating, slicing and dicing the truth; in other words, lying. He spent no little amount of time debunking the god of autobiographical reverence in his students.

I was Morris's teaching assistant, a job that helped pay my out-of-state tuition at San Francisco State University (a college in 1965), which involved taking attendance in his huge lecture class The Craft of Fiction and listening in his office to his hysterically funny impersonations of his colleagues and fellow writers. Some of these writers—Saul Bellow, Bernard Malamud, Katherine Anne Porter, Kay Boyle, and Peter Taylor—were heroes of mine, and enjoying his stories was a lot easier than keeping attendance for him, which meant having to maneuver down steeply inclined auditorium aisles and walkways while counting heads on an attendance sheet. I had good reason to fear tripping on something and maybe rolling down one of the steep aisles. For one thing, given the way just about everyone there kept sneaking looks at me and sniggering, it was clear what they were hoping would happen. It wasn't that they sought a distraction from what Wright was saying, he was highly entertaining and his classes were as popular as any in the English department. It perhaps had something to do with the adamancy with which I went about counting heads and checking my attendance sheet, or the fact that I was agile enough to seemingly hop over obstacles suspiciously left in my path with little notice or complaint. But, as everyone knew, Wright did insist on knowing who wasn't interested enough in his thoughts about Saul Bellow, Edith Wharton, and Twain to attend and when I actually did trip on something someone left in the walkway, and rolled halfway down the ramp to within a foot of where Wright stood at the podium looking down at me with that Nebraskan prairie twinkle of incredulity in his blue eyes, everyone clapped and roared their approval, even before Wright said: "Dear Mr. Schultz, please understand it's best to win attention through one's work, not antics."

I had, among other reasons, come to San Francisco to study with him, having been recommended to do so at my previous college, the University of Louisville, by a renowned critic/teacher, Harvey Curtis Webster, who believed him to be, after Saul Bellow, our most important American novelist. It was fiction I was most interested in then, and his response to the first story I showed him has remained the most memorable. The story was over twenty pages, some typed while others were handwritten in my unintelligible dyslexic script, and when I proudly informed him that I'd written it all the night before in a fever of inspiration, he nodded and, placing a wastebasket between us, motioned for me to sit down across from him. It was still light and the view of the ocean sunset outside his office window was striking. He worked with a chosen few (many of my fellow students were afraid to work with him) and I understood it was a privilege to have to wait two weeks for an appointment to discuss my work for twenty or so minutes and was expecting the kind of praise I'd gotten in the past from my other instructors.

Pausing to light up one of his famous Marsh Wheeling cigars, he smiled and said, "So you put all of a few minutes of your precious time in these fevered reminiscences of childhood and now expect more than a few minutes of mine in responding to them, is that correct?"

It was all I could do to nod as he slowly raised one of my pages to the tip of his cigar, and, giving me ample time to object, carefully lit it. Too stricken to speak, let alone protest, I watched what only moments before I believed to be a work of inspired brilliance ignite and burn, page after page, against the glow of the gathering dusk.

Then, dropping the still-burning pages into the wastebasket, he sighed and said, "Writing well takes concentrated, strenuous effort. Inspiration occasionally makes an appearance, but never trust it. My dear boy, next time show me something you've worked on."

Given how stubbornly impulsive and passionate I was, he probably assumed nothing less dramatic would work. Though I've never done anything like this with any of my students, it's necessary to remember that this was the mid-Sixties in San Francisco, when revolution and youthful spontaneity were the presiding gods, each often enough induced by chemical intervention. In any case, it worked; I never ever again showed him or anyone else a rough draft of anything I wrote. And he was patient and affectionate with me to a fault thereafter; of the many valuable things I learned from him, the most memorable is the degree of skepticism and objectivity with which he viewed all stories, his own and others', believing that since most writers weren't quite as smart as they wanted themselves and others to believe, it was better to ask questions than attempt to answer them, and that embellishment was often a sign of laziness and incompetence. But what I took to heart was his belief that our most extraordinary asset was our ordinariness, the ways in which we were like everyone else, and the qualities of sympathy and insight that join us. I may not recall every word he ever said to me, but I remember enough and only many years later did I understand what he meant when he said our stories never really belong to us, they belong to anyone curious and kind enough to listen to or read them, and that it's what we say about others that is most relevant and revealing of ourselves. Wright, who shared my birthday and always sent a card reminding me of the fact for many years afterward, believed each version of what we write is an opportunity to reinvent ourselves, and say something that might outlast our impatience and ignorance by an hour, day, or lifetime. He believed too, I remember, that we don't have to like or even trust our narrators; we just have to believe them.

Wright delighted in impersonating his best and favorite creation, his bemused, ironic persona narrator forever muddling his way through often-incomprehensible experiences. Writers were entertainers, he believed, their characters seriocomic actors in stories devised to reflect the aspirations and absurdities of their time, not stand-ins for autobiographical selves relating experiences that happened only to them. My persona often enough sees himself as a vaguely familiar oddity trapped in an improbable situation he has no idea how to extricate himself from, other than by turning the ineffable into written language. In other words, I too suffer what I see. Many years later his dictum, I Came, I Saw, I Suffered, took on a new and galvanizing meaning for me. All writers have secret agendas, mixed unconscious feelings concerning important incidents in our lives that we insist we understand well enough to write about, when in fact our cluelessness is not only the state we exist in but also our real subject, at least as a starting place. In many instances the whole point of serious writing is to discover exactly what this cluelessness is hiding, which is often a conflict too painful to adjudicate or lay bare without further creative effort. My job as a teacher is similar to what I do as a writer, unravel these conflicts and secret agendas into successful work, to help make the peculiar commonplace and maybe even somewhat endearing, which is a long and complicated process.

I used to believe pointing this out was perhaps my purpose and mission as a writer and teacher, but my wife, Monica, sees another more immediate and practical benefit. She believes our real contribution as artists is the manner in which we encourage and inspire the kind of self-knowledge that can serve as a shield against despair. That in providing a place where people, who are also parents, spouses, and every kind of professional, can think creatively, we are also giving them the agency to be independent of their biases and worries long enough to thrive not only as writers but as human beings. The dictionary, she pointed out, gives the verb "to express" two distinct meanings: "to set forth the opinions, feelings, etc., of oneself, as in speaking, writing or painting, and to press or squeeze out: to express the juice of grapes, to exude or emit a liquid, odor, as if under pressure: the roses expressed a sweet perfume." Monica, a gifted and successful sculptor, has from the beginning seen technical proficiency and critique as values for self-acceptance and the very idea of expression can engender a sense of freedom from daily restraints and obligations. Indeed, art isn't in the business of giving absolution or even comfort. When asked if writing or her own process-oriented art, sculpture, offers emotional catharsis she replies no, it's a way of using her emotions as raw material to explore the personal, private, impractical, useless aspects of herself.

I was recently asked after a reading I gave who I wrote for, what kind of reader I aimed at. After hesitating, I said that the reader I wanted most to please is myself, that I try to write the kind of poem and book I most enjoy reading. It's that simple? the person asked. Yes, I said, that simple and impossible. Such questions are the hardest to answer. I'm not an expert of any kind and don't enjoy being seen as one. The person looked disappointed, hoping for something perhaps a little more magnificent, or at least esoteric. But good writers write the kind of books they want to read, beyond that it's all accident and luck. On its most basic level writing is a selfish act. It isn't altruism or philanthropy, and I'm not really a salesman, a preacher, or a social worker; occasionally, it's pleasurable and I enjoy seeing myself as someone others might come to admire, but what I really am is an interloper, an intruder into inner sanctums, a collaborator, and a trespasser. In the unspoken bargain between writer and reader it's understood that all sorts of boundaries will be crossed, and private selves intruded upon. The disappointment being risked on both parts is profound: the failure to confront in oneself that which remains too strong, intimidating, and opaque to be realized.

Is this why I feel so helpless every time I begin to write and must tolerate so absurd and fraudulent a feeling when confronting what I perceive as yet another attempt to render the unimaginable plausible? Why, for instance, after attending a memorial service recently for someone I didn't know personally, a lawyer who wrote our will, I came home dejected, unable to do anything but lie on my chartreuse couch in my study wondering what people might say about me at such an occasion? Yes, a rather morbid response to what I found to be a moving event, in which the wife and daughter of the deceased seemed so comfortable with their feelings of love and grief they were able to make fun of themselves and him in front of a large crowd of friends, family, and colleagues. He appeared to be loved and admired by many for his generosity toward the less fortunate and keen sense of community. What would people say about me at such an event, I wondered, spending as I do so much of my life holed up in my study, writing out of some personal grievance and inner turmoil about nearly everything that ever happened to me—what did I contribute to my community, if anything at all?

The man's confident, openhearted daughter sang "Hey Jude" with everyone joining in for the chorus, humming and singing along with her. The intensity with which she ended her song turned this solemn event into a concert of appreciation and lament, which I then managed to turn into a jury trial in which I tried but couldn't name one good, acceptable quality I owned that others might mourn. The fact that it was Father's Day and I was about to be celebrated by my family made me feel only more wretched. Above all else, the shitbird hates the very thinking and feeling it inspires; hates even the possibility that one can stumble across the truth by mistake, and whatever satisfaction and happiness might arise out of it. It may be because my early life was such a maze of fantasies, distortions, and exaggeration that everything I write is on some level an attempt to see myself as others may see me, to believe I'm worthy of some modicum of respect.

Begin each story, Hemingway tells us in *A Moveable Feast*, with one true sentence. In other words, the more important a subject, the more daunting and curious its process of discovery; if the truth and style are there, the meaning will find a way to surface.

This process often starts with an idea we want to explore further, and then proceeds to a style that leads us to an emotion, which, if genuine enough, takes us to a more profound level of meaning. Each step of this process is a complicated conundrum that demands absolute attention, patience, and tolerance of the anxiety and disappointment that so often accompany it.

The black bird wants us to worry about end results, who will publish what, how well something will be received, using wild-goose chases, ambivalence, and detours as obstacles and distraction. If what we create is to be of some small use or inspiration to others, and thereby serve as encouragement and comfort, this process should include the reader. Is this sentence, idea, line, and metaphor clear enough, understandable—how might someone very different from me, of another proficiency altogether, react to this? It's so easy to become entangled in our own personal prejudices and aspirations to the point of failing to recognize that we're actually speaking to others. Yes, we may be writing for ourselves, but at some essential level we're also attempting to communicate with strangers, to render the unfamiliar plausible, worthy of their consideration and sympathy.

Serious writers are archaeologists of their emotional and spiritual lives, risk-takers willing to excavate what lies hidden in our most private selves, especially since what is found there is seldom particularly agreeable, or welcoming. Creative writing is essentially an intervention on behalf of the self, an overlapping of intentions and desires, which is never convenient or completely controlled by any party. Illusions must often be confronted, sacrificed, and abandoned; in changing, we each encounter some facet or quality of ourselves that renders us vulnerable to profound wonder and disappointment. In a sense we are always learning anew what it is we came for, what we saw, and therefore, what we suffered.

IN THE MANNER OF POETRY

The personas we select for ourselves, for our personalities, encompass a long, semiconscious process that entails necessity, fear, and accommodation, if not a certain degree of subterfuge, while the ones we use in our work involve mostly ambition, astuteness, and a desire to both expose and camouflage our more private intentions, if not selves. In order to extend our imagination beyond that point where we may feel safe to go, our poetic personas often require the kind of self-knowledge, objectivity, and desire we can find only in the personas of those writers we select as models. In either case, an awareness of the nature of the negativity we're being tested by is essential.

The first and perhaps most enduring poetic model I chose, without fully being aware of the fact, was the one George Oppen devised for both his person and his work. An objectivist poet, he became my mentor and guide in San Francisco in 1968, a heady and demanding time in which men in my position, unable to find full-time work because of our tenuous draft situation, wandered around campuses and other such places, looking for spontaneity and its distractions. I met George after a poetry reading he gave at San Francisco State University, which I'd graduated from the previous spring. Poetry readings were then ubiquitous in the Bay Area, but not poetry readings like his, in which every word and punctuation mark felt hard-earned and inevitable. I was mesmerized by his use of clarity and sophisticated philosophical and political observation and immediately knew that this was the way I also wanted to write, with conviction and great emotional directness. I was still leaning toward fiction but his persona, which appeared to care little for allusion, myth, and even metaphor and simile, seemed to be wrought out of the strict-hewn texture of his being. Like Hemingway's, his persona was that of a stoic aesthete stripped of all guile and discernible ideology or literary affectation, indifferent to appearances and detectable fashions. He read his work simply, never performing it, as nearly everyone else in the Bay Area did, often with great fanfare. l could think of no one writer he sounded like, or appeared influenced by, his every word spoken in a rather flat, take-it-or-leave-it style, as if challenging anyone to doubt the veracity of a single syllable.

I managed to stick around long enough after the reading to meet him and we walked across campus together to the trolley back to the city, past all the political booths and merry-making Zen thespians and obsessed ideologists of every stripe. "Ah, the lovely absurdity of youth," he laughed, managing somehow to include me in all this jubilance. Yes, I thought, I *was* part of all this, and, to some extent, writers like George were our chroniclers, translating all this energy and mayhem into coded anthems for everyone else to enjoy and decipher. But it was his honesty I liked, the fact that he didn't mince words or thoughts. "I liked even what I didn't understand in your poems," I told him as we waited for the trolley back to the city, "it's not like anything I've ever read or heard before."

He asked if I was a student there and I explained that I had been and had also recently been a graduate student in poetry at the University of Iowa but had returned here after only three and a half months. When he asked why, I said I'd realized I wasn't really suited to be a graduate student, and even though not being in school meant facing the terrible prospect of Vietnam, I or the writer in me seemed to need to be here, in what felt like the real world.

"So you're in a kind of self-exile out here," he smiled, "not knowing what to do next?"

"Yes, I have no idea what comes next."

We both smiled at the thought, and then sighed audibly.

"Well, I've been there myself. I'm also from the East Coast. We have a few things in common."

He invited me to dinner at his house in North Beach that Friday night and over the course of the next few years I enjoyed many dinners with him and his wife, Mary, always, it seemed, on a Friday night. It was a coincidence no doubt, I thought, that two secular Jews should always pick a Sabbath night to meet. He was of German Jewish descent and I of Russian and Polish descent, and he knew firsthand what living in an uncertain state of exile was like. He'd been wounded while a foot soldier in WWII, winning a Purple Heart, though, as he said many times, his was a vastly different and necessary war. For seven years, he and Mary had survived the terrors of McCarthyism while hiding out in Mexico, and he seemed especially attuned to the fact that I was without family support and on the run amid what seemed the ever-growing chaos of the times. His childhood was privileged and he had enjoyed a small but sustainable inheritance, but his political affinities (he had been a Communist activist for much of his youth) had also led him to a life of manual labor, working as a carpenter, printer, furniture maker, and tool-and-die mechanic in Mexico and elsewhere, while I got by on part-time jobs driving a cab, working on the docks, and, for a very short time, driving a trolley elevator from the bowels of Twin Peaks to the street. And like him, I too appeared to live in a world at least somewhat constructed out of my imagination. During our walks along the San Francisco Bay, he'd explain the benefits of finding a woman like Mary and eventually settling down somewhere less frantic so I could concentrate on my work. He warned me against the attractions and convolutions of what he called the Eastern Literary Establishment, which he felt distrustful of because of its ardent social contract and politics, its emphasis on traditional dogmas and careerism. He knew and admired poets like Ezra Pound, whose fascist beliefs he abhorred even if he understood why Pound had embraced them, and who wrote an introduction to his first book, *Discrete Series*, in 1934, published by the Objectivist Press, which George put out with his fellow Communists and outliers, Charles Reznikoff, Carl Rakosi, and Louis Zukofsky. He would boast about smuggling a banned copy of James Joyce's *Ulysses* through customs into the States from Paris in a suitcase, reading Pound for the first time in London, and the importance of his sometimes contentious and mutually affectionate friendship with William Carlos Williams—Doc, he called him—who befriended him at a time when everything seemed new and overwhelming, as they now did for me. He talked at great length about Williams, Pound, and Eliot and I remember vividly his stuttering descriptions of the paradox of his being a Communist living off a trust fund provided by his capitalist father, the great upheavals and contradictions of life lived at full stride, and the apprehensions of life on the fringes of one's knowledge and beliefs. His father, he explained, had shortened their name from Oppenheimer—J. Robert Oppenheimer, the lead scientist running the Manhattan Project in Los Alamos, New Mexico, which created the first atomic bomb, was, apparently, George's second cousin on, oddly enough, his mother's side—and perhaps that too factored into the profound and engaging sadness I felt in his presence, that and his mother's suicide when he was four, a sadness that could be seen in the very crags of his long serious features and measured gaze. He was a great humanist poet who advised me on many essential subjects and though I wouldn't understand much of what he told me, especially about poetry, for another twenty years, I appreciated the warmth and generosity of his attention.

What I did understand almost immediately after meeting him was that he was the perfect embodiment of what I imagined a writer to be: someone whose complete being is the personification of an artist, not someone playing the role in bearing, manner, and costume, but someone for whom such things are as inevitable as what he or she produces; someone who had no choice in the matter and had earned the right to call themselves one.

In particular I remember the Friday night after dinner when he took me into his narrow study to show me his desk (where every pencil and paperclip seemed to hold a place of honor) and pointed to typewritten pages of poems intensely inscribed with notes carefully written around words and phrases and in the margins. I had no way of knowing how many drafts these lines represented, though I imagined many more than I could ever bring myself to do. And when he explained that no matter how tired or distracted he was, he'd always reread a few lines of what he'd written that day before going to bed, feeling confident that whatever problem he'd experienced would be resolved by the morning, I tried to imagine my unconscious mind finishing a poem while I slept, advice that many years later helped me while I was struggling to finish my novel in verse, *The Wherewithal*. Before going to bed, I'd sit at the dining room table, interrogating myself about what I would write the next morning, knowing that if I didn't my anxiety would be too great in the morning to write, praying that by immersing myself in the very darkness I was writing about (the Holocaust, the Vietnam War, and the welfare system in San Francisco in the Sixties) I would *see* and *feel* the history I was confronting. More than once I felt George's presence during these nights, though I doubt he would've approved of the shots of vodka I drank as insulation and false encouragement.

According to George, a poem was done when every last comma and period was in its proper place—every single one. When I showed him one of my poems, he'd marvel at a single word or image, ignoring everything else I'd worked so hard on. One decent line or half-formed image was something to praise in someone my age, he said and though it would hurt to realize all thirty or forty of my other lines were less than memorable, I understood how lucky I was to have a teacher who would point out what no one else I knew could. He may not have thought of himself as a teacher (he was never one in any formal sense), but his generosity and forbearance were qualities that clearly came naturally to him and the pleasure he took in encouraging me made a lasting impression.

There's a good reason why George used this Martin Heidegger quote "the arduous path of appearance" as an epigraph for his third book of poetry, *This in Which*. Appearances to George were the kind of superficialities and indulgences he deemed dangerous to poetry; any reliance on fluency in language struck him, as it did Wright Morris, as contrived and willed emotion. If even a hint of it appeared in a poem I showed him he'd shake his head and sigh, and then find a different word or two to compliment. Language itself should be held suspect, he believed, since it too often called attention to its devices, and self-consciously held itself up as a paradigm. Language was a means of communication, a servant to the meaning it strove to convey, nothing more. Once it conveyed its meaning and music, its job was complete. Poetry derived from the rigors of hard-earned-and-wrought thought and emotion stripped of anything designed to impress. Fashion impressed, not ideas; ideas convinced and described, and if they managed to occasionally move readers with their seriousness and susceptibility to interpretation all the better. It was us we should strive to impress and no one else, and we should therefore be the hardest and most withholding of all our readers. When he liked even a phrase or line of anything I wrote I saw it as a great achievement.

George was the product of his thinking, and his thinking was the result of what he'd suffered and survived. In 1969 he won the Pulitzer Prize for *Of Being Numerous*, the title poem an indictment of the Vietnam War, which he was writing during the time I knew him. I returned to Iowa in 1970 and though we lost touch in the following years his friendship remained a continuing source of encouragement. When I heard of George's death in 1983, I was reminded of Robert Musil's description of his own aesthetic as being "toward the severe." When Musil was asked if he, like so many other serious writers, didn't want a larger audience—his novel, *The Man without Qualities*, was one everyone familiar with European literature knew about but few actually read—his reply seemed also a good description of George's aesthetic: "I am not the kind of author who tells his readers what they want to hear because they know it anyway. . . . My readers have gradually come to me, not I to them." As with George, everything was subordinated to his sense of "passionate seriousness," a seriousness that knew how to survive not only war and exile but also the passion of despair and conscience.

This arduous seriousness and strict disregard for appearances, or fashion of any sort, were aspects of his persona I so ardently adapted to my own, as a person, as a poet, and later as a teacher. I certainly used his example when structuring the poems in my first book out of what at times felt like the whole cloth of my imagination. If I were to err as a writer it would be on the side of truth and stupidity, not ambition and whimsy. When deciding on how to proceed in a particularly challenging subject, I would remember his lessons on my developing as a writer slowly and accurately, without assuming too much or placing too much emphasis on personal identification. Writers develop at their own pace, with their reading being the sole source of inspiration and ambition. This certainly helped with my own work.

Whenever I find myself taken with the fluency of any aspect of a poem I've written I'll stop myself and then put it aside until that time when I can bear to look at it more objectively, with the confidence of a greater reserve. Much and most of what I write is filler, partially considered ideas and exhortations devised to appeal to those instincts I've learned to distrust, even disdain. When I reach that point in a poem beyond which I can neither add nor subtract context or inclination, I know I've reached the place where George lived most of his poetic life, a place that asked for nothing more of the reader than what he'd earned in respect and credibility, a place neither particularly kind nor remunerating, though where true satisfaction lived. His manner, though generous and even cautiously modest at times, was always manifestly critical in the most positive and constructive sense. It's through the discerning filter of his eyes that my persona observes the various drafts of my poems and, to some extent, my life.

This is section 8 from George's poem "Route," from *Of Being Numerous*.

> Cars on the highway filled with speech,
> People talk, they talk to each other;
>
> Imagine a man in the ditch,
> The wheels of the overturned wreck
> Still spinning—

I don't mean he despairs, I mean if he does not
He sees in the manner of poetry

Thinking in the manner of poetry changes not only the writer but also the world he or she perceives. There are no appearances in reality, and once embraced, the imagination changes everything else.

A NEW CITY OF WORDS

J ohn Cheever once described in some detail the sense of alienation his being drunk created. We were taking one of our eight-
mile Sunday bike rides near his house in Ossining, New York,
and he was telling me about a time when he often seemed to be
watching himself from across a room, wondering who this man was
and why he was behaving so curiously. Usually just cranking our old
bikes around the winding Hudson Valley hill roads was more than
enough activity, but he seemed determined to talk about this and
the strain in his voice was audible over the wind and our breathing. More often his stories concerned his illustrious writer friends,
Saul Bellow, John Updike, and Philip Roth, and the poets he knew
I admired, Robert Lowell, W. S. Merwin, and Elizabeth Bishop, but
not this Sunday. I wouldn't have liked him if I'd known him when
he was drinking, he said, and he was right. I'd once, years before I
met him, seen him drunk in a Provincetown restaurant, carrying on
loudly across the room, and I clearly remember promising myself to
never let myself get to that mindless state, certainly not in public.
The place was filled with writers and artists and we all knew who he
was, and he knew we all did. It was a painful performance to watch,
one he most definitely didn't seem to be watching or listening to.

We met at Yaddo, in 1975, where he, a celebrity writer who was
recently "famously sober," as one painter there put it, seemed to

be table-hopping at dinner each night, looking for lively company. My table, I imagined, with its collection of artists and writers of varying ages and levels of social inhibitions, offered just the kind of merriment he preferred and when he joined us, he stared directly at me, as if challenging me to make him laugh, along with the others at the table. Well, what I said made everyone but him laugh, at least at first. I said, "I have to say I love your work. *Rabbit, Run* is one of my favorite novels."

As if not quite sure how good-natured my remark was, he first looked somewhat curiously at me, and then smiled and said, "Actually, my own favorite is *Portnoy's Complaint*, it certainly sold better."

Laughter became a mainstay in our friendship. Having taught "The Country Husband" and "The Enormous Radio" several times, I truly admired his stories, and he seemed appreciative of what he saw as my rather cavalier attitude toward my penurious state, derived, he believed, from my haphazard immigrant survival instincts, which he deduced from my dinner-table stories, once telling someone in my presence that I not only didn't have a pot to piss in, I didn't seem to mind or even know it. He was referring, I understood later, to the persona I presented—a mishmash, I supposed, of Hemingway's and my father's bravado and fiercely guarded vulnerability, and a more personal, principled belief in vindication and providential rewards—which perhaps seemed familiar to him, given that to some degree his own presented a somewhat similar attitude and disposition, and he perhaps enjoyed the idea that I was actively living out a scenario he may have once imagined for himself. After he asked to see my poems and told me he very much liked them, our friendship changed again. The crosscurrents of friendship are mystifying, and perhaps unknowable, but the "I" I saw through his eyes nourished me during a time when everything seemed to be off-kilter and changing at a dizzying rate. No sooner would I survive one badly matched and unreasoned relationship than I'd find another one even more ill-suited. When I moved to Manhattan in 1976 and started visiting him in Ossining, I would occasionally bring a lady friend up for Sunday lunch and John and his wife, Mary, would find opportunities to comment on their suitability for me. Mary once shyly pointed out in the kitchen that one young lady seemed, though charming, more interested in the idea of me as a poet than as a viable partner, which could cause trouble after a while. Her observation, which I promptly ignored, turned out to be true.

The persona John presented seemed a kind of front man for someone less considered, who was working very hard to make the correct impression. It was fun hearing him speak in what sounded at times like a British accent, favoring miscellaneous and fastidious words, like "estimable," which he gave as high praise for something produced at great personal cost, and "balmy," which could mean soothing, calm, or crazy, depending on what or whom he was describing. "Splendid," his favorite, covered anything from a rich sunset to talent and someone's bearing, including his own, which often appeared rather aristocratic and "splendidly" stoic. At times he'd poke fun at this apparent facade, which only made his larger personality seem all the more elusive and fascinating. He enjoyed, for instance, hearing himself say how much he detested a writer he knew back in Boston who apparently went around boasting that he'd known John before he had an accent, which meant, I assumed, that he'd known John before he'd acquired his fancy Brahmin, and at times rather studied, manners. The fact that nobody I knew had ever heard of his insulter and couldn't have cared less about what he said didn't faze John in the least. His persona believed it clever and perhaps virtuous to be perceived as repeating an insult made at his expense. This penchant for wit at any cost no doubt influenced my own attitude toward how seriously I should take myself, especially when he'd scoff if I said something that sounded even remotely self-pitying.

I didn't understand the degree to which this persona allowed him to survive not only the solitary regimen of his discipline as a writer but the pain of his dissolute and drunken escapes from it. The fact that my persona was so different and similar in so many perplexing ways may be why the more vulnerable I appeared the more determined he and Mary were to help me succeed; as Mary once put it, the more desperate my stories, the funnier they were. She once dedicated a poem to me that dealt with a brave tailor stitching words as he sets out toward "the dark forest." It was called "Courage" and at the bottom she wrote the dates Autumn 1976– Autumn 1979 to indicate how long she'd worked on it. The tailor's journey into "a new city of words / Buildings lookouts and strongholds" was the dark forest she saw me setting out into, one she and John both knew only too well. I spent many Sundays, holidays, and birthdays at their house and once Mary affectionately referred to me as an "adoptable naïf." I imagine I was that and more. But their kindness during these years when everything seemed to be beginning, mostly for the good, meant a great deal to me.

John wrote my publisher, Viking Press, insisting they publish my first book, *Like Wings*, which came out the same year, 1978, as his collected stories, *The Stories of John Cheever*, and he then went around promoting both books. Both were nominated for National Book Awards and though neither won, his book went on to win the Pulitzer Prize the following year. The morning the National Book Awards were announced he called to say neither of us had won, but "wasn't it great fun while it lasted?" Great fun, indeed! When the *New Yorker* took one of my poems, he'd call to say they were finally showing some literary acumen, and when a poem was rejected, he'd say that they clearly didn't know what they were doing. It was a good time for both of us and the fact that we were sharing it made it all the more special. In every instance, he seemed more excited for me than he was for himself. We were both, in our own ways, possessed by personas that now dominated every facet of our actual personalities. At times it seemed as if I were being introduced to mine all over again in a vain attempt to modify and reduce any further risk of failure, and it was during this time of good news that someone began calling every night at exactly four in the morning and not saying a word.

"Hello, hello? Who's there?" I'd yell, fearing it was someone I'd somehow slighted or made jealous. Friends pleaded with me to disconnect my phone before going to sleep—it was that simple, all I had to do was disconnect my phone to end what had become an endless nightmare. But I kept answering it, and then would go through the day feeling as if I'd been identified in a police lineup for a crime in which I was both the accuser and the victim. But on some level, I must've known who was calling: my old friend the shitbird. And after I finally stopped answering it and the calls ended, I wasn't surprised when John also started behaving strangely. The day before a reading I helped arrange for him at the 92nd Street Y in Manhattan (with the generous help of Grace Schulman, the fine poet and then director of the reading series) he managed to shut a car door on his hand and called that night to say he didn't think he could go through with it. He let me convince him that he could, and then read with a bandaged hand, and at dinner afterward spoke at length of a woman who had sat at the back of the large auditorium, scowling. The fact that the place was packed to overflowing with adoring fans didn't deter him from noticing only this one woman, a neighbor in Ossining whom he didn't particularly like.

When I asked why anyone would travel all the way from Ossining to the Upper East Side only to scowl derisively, couldn't she just do it locally, he just shrugged. Sunk deeply in a well-upholstered funk, he'd compressed all of us into one phantom visage—wasn't this, I wondered, the deal he'd made with his shitbird that allowed him to balance and then tolerate his own brilliance, the genius necessary to so thoroughly delight and enliven so many readers for so long? It brought to mind an exercise he gave his writing students: write a scene in which someone has to escape a burning building. Knowing that many young writers try to avoid dramatic conflict, he was asking them to create a third-person narrator whose only job was to describe the actions of a character under great duress, which meant "seeing" themselves as characters reacting to an emergency without backstory, analysis, flashbacks, or reminiscences; their one task was to relate what their characters did to escape. Wasn't this what he was doing now, creating a persona narrator who would allow him to escape the emergency of gratitude and affection? This was how he diminished the firestorm of acknowledgment without the help of booze, or as he might put it, *The Sorrows of Gin*.

Another idea he gave me also became an exercise I used in my classes: the way in which he sometimes created a lively third-person narrator by first creating a successful first-person one he would then use to tell another character's story. Some of his best third-person persona narrators were made this way, he said. The third-person narrator of his great story "The Country Husband" made the kind of disapproving comments about his main character, Francis, more characteristic of a first-person narrator. "Francis, taking off his hat and putting down his paper, was not consciously pleased with the scene; he was not that reflective." "Flavorful" was the word he used to describe this narrative quality; a narrator had to be flavorful enough to make his characters come alive in an interesting manner and most of his first-person narrators were exactly that—so why not use them as third-person narrators? I now ask students to do precisely that: turn first-person narrators into third-person ones, which isn't unlike a ventriloquist being seen and spoken about by his dummy, a point of view that demands a more original use of one's imagination.

"THE NOBILITY IN HIS WORK," John once said about Hemingway's work. "His narrators are so noble, and refined, I always admired that!" This was after telling me that Hemingway's widow, Mary, had once told him at a New York party that her husband liked his story "Goodbye, My Brother" enough to wake her late one night to read it to her in its entirety. They were at home in San Francisco de Paula, Cuba, and, having just read it in the *New Yorker*, Hemingway thought it as good as anything he'd read in a long time. As good as Chekhov, he apparently told her. And since he seldom said anything like this, she wanted John to know it. John's story, his most personal and hauntingly passionate, was about his relationship with his older brother, Fred, told in the voice of a first-person narrator who could no longer tolerate the darkness of his older brother's perverse nature. At the end of the story, in surrender, he says of his brother, "Oh, what can you do with a man like that? How can you dissuade his eye in a crowd from seeking out the cheek with acne, the infirm hand; how can you teach him to respond to the inestimable greatness of the race, the hard surface beauty of life; how can you put his finger for him on the obdurate truths before which fear and horror are powerless?"

This is as good a description of the shitbird as I can imagine and seeing how John stepped in and out of its shadow not only helped me understand my own relationship to mine, it also explained what occurred during my first visit to his house, when, after picking me up at the train station, he'd seemed both agitated and preoccupied. As we walked to his car, he explained that his brother Fred had died a few days ago and that he probably wasn't very good company. I expressed sympathy and offered to return to the city if he preferred to be alone. No, no, after coming up from the city I should stay at least for lunch, he said. I did stay and after lunch, still seated at his dining room table, he began telling me about their relationship, which was fraught with rivalry and disdain, especially at the end of his brother's life, he said. He was always trying to win Fred's approval, and often they didn't speak for long periods of time. I was familiar with his famous story about his brother and was intrigued when he began talking about their boyhoods in Quincy, Massachusetts, and later as young men living on Hudson Street in Manhattan. And now he was speaking quietly in a flat monotone, to no one in particular, it seemed, to perhaps only himself or some imagined presence—a reader?—his words flowing with such musical fervor and urgency I no longer felt uncomfortable in hearing such intimate stories from someone I didn't as yet know well. I felt the way I did when reading his stories, as if I were there, watching it all happen before my eyes. It seemed magical. A moment earlier, he was solemn and somewhat discomfited, as if he were being browbeaten by his older brother, but now he spoke of the distinct, *estimable* lives of brothers with such intensity of emotion I found myself overcome with grief, and, unable to control myself, I began to weep.

He stopped talking, and looked at me, curiously.

So this was how he wrote, I thought, he disappeared into his persona, who, knowing its job, took over, shielding him from further harm. All he required was a reader, a listener, to feel what perhaps he otherwise could or would not.

It was clear that I was weeping for both of us.

There wasn't much more conversation. He took me to the train station and shook my hand and wished me well.

"I hope I didn't bore you with all that. I did go on for a while."

Still shaken, not knowing what to say, I said nothing, for which he appeared grateful and reassured.

The following week there was another invitation, and the week after that, another one. It appeared we had become friends.

ANGER AND SHAME

Every strong creative impulse creates a cautionary reaction just as strong, and the more intimate and difficult our subject matter, the greater and more turbulent the reaction—is this why I so fear acknowledging in my work the harm and transgressions I may have caused, what might be revealed even in my successes? It's most certainly why I demand of myself some awareness of the process in which I'm so thoroughly engaged, why I interrogate myself at every step of the creative journey. It's also why I ask my students, before reading their work in class, to present preambles or statements in which they reiterate the criticism they heard the previous week, explain how they applied it, and then ask a question that best indicates what issue most preoccupied them during the writing. This question often proves the most challenging part and what I mostly hear back are general proclamations: whether there's a persona narrator present, or whether the mood or tone they were after is apparent. Few students ever ask the question so many writers find the most compelling and troubling: who may be hurt or offended by what they are writing. Joan Didion put this fear best in the preface to *Slouching towards Bethlehem*: "*Writers are always selling somebody out.*" At some point every writer must deal with a similar question: Do we deserve satisfaction for causing pain to others, especially those we love?

Eugene O'Neill didn't allow what I consider his best play, *Long Day's Journey into Night*, which dealt with his most intimate and volatile feelings about his immediate family, to be published until twenty-five years after his death; Eudora Welty and Katherine Anne Porter waited until the end of their writing lives to deal with the potently complex situations and characters drawn from their personal histories in *Losing Battles* and *Ship of Fools*. To protect others and, ultimately, themselves, many writers meticulously disguise their characters and sometimes postpone essential material indefinitely. And in my experience, anger is the emotion that is most often hidden behind this fear of self-incrimination, retribution, and insensitivity toward others. Anger and the shame it so often creates; the shame we feel for being angry at those we love. Maybe especially when anger is the appropriate response in a story or poem, it's seldom easily found; in fact, in otherwise finely orchestrated student work, it's often impossible to detect. And when I ask for the emotional truth in a scene or in lines of poetry, what I most often hear are excuses, apologies, and static of all kinds. Yes, anger is what the majority of my students most stridently avoid and/or refuse to recognize in their work and sometimes in the work of others, even when its absence is glaringly obvious to me and many others.

One writer who ran away from home as a teenager and was forever trying to find her way back in her writing couldn't access the anger that made her leave home in the first place; another couldn't overcome the depths of her anger and shame in writing about a gay father who she felt had abandoned her as a child, and the ways in which this anger effected her eventual destruction of her family and herself as an adult; the union activist unafraid to take on tough factory bosses in standing up for workers' rights but unable to do the same against a domineering father; a writer so indoctrinated in spousal abandonments she stops writing just as she reaches the limits of her perceived allowance of indignation and success. Some, it would seem, would rather fail at what means most to them, their creative work, than confront painful truths, anger being, from my experience, the hardest to recognize and acknowledge. The imagination thrives on powerful emotions, and discovering what we're actually feeling under all the more stately and comfortable emotions we disguise them with can be a source of creative inspiration and thinking. Of its many forms and disguises, anger can be seen as reproach and instigation, a setting of boundaries and constraints, a system of checks and balances, a vow, and a warning system so sophisticated and subtle we learn to both fear and appreciate its undeniable forecasts. And shame, what we so often feel in its wake, equally dominates and restricts our choice of subject matter and desire to confront shameful truths.

As Cioran said, "A negative habit is fruitful only so long as we exert ourselves to overcome it, adapt it to our needs." Writers learn to live with anxiety and exhilaration the way athletes learn to live with pain, yet so many of my students highlight a less menacing emotion at the expense of a more powerful one, which so disrupts their sense of equilibrium. And when anger's absence—that special rush of liquid fire—is obvious to everyone except the writer, I sometimes ask what the other students might feel if placed in the same position as the writer's narrator or character. Consensus of opinion provides not only verification but also the sense of solidarity and commiseration necessary to approach painful material. Even when camouflaged or diluted with satire and comedy, I'll point out, anger is prominent in many of the great works we study in craft class: Ginsberg's "Howl," Philip Larkin's "This Be the Verse," Yeats's "The Second Coming" and "Easter 1916" ("What is it but nightfall? / No, no, not night but death; / Wasn't it needless death after all?"), and Blake's "Morning" ("To Find the Western path / Right thro' the Gates of Wrath / I urge my way"); in Shakespeare's

Hamlet, Ralph Ellison's *Invisible Man*, James Baldwin's *The Fire Next Time*, and Dante's revenge fantasies in *The Inferno*. Writers are in the business of divulging secrets, confessing to shames and regrets, but doing so often means using oneself as an example, as Keats does so powerfully in "Ode on a Grecian Urn."

Yes, Keats knew how emotionally expensive the exquisiteness of beauty and truth were to attain. Is this why it's not "possible to live in the bare present," as Martin Buber tells us in *I and Thou*, because the present would "consume" us if we didn't take precautions to defend ourselves against it? Why we can live only in "the bare past," where life can be organized, tolerated, and enjoyed? Keats would've agreed with Buber that writing is a way of organizing the past well enough to find meaning in the present, where most of us want to live, even though it's where most of our pain and anger also reside. In that it makes us honest witnesses to our own acts of self-betrayal, suffering can be redemptive. And Keats had much to be angry about.

These lines are written on his tombstone in Rome: "This grave contains all that was mortal of a young English poet who on his death-bed in the bitterness of his heart at the malicious power of his enemies desired these words to be engraved on his tombstone: Here lies One Whose Name was writ in Water." He died of consumption at the age of twenty-five, having suffered scalding reviews of his work and perhaps, in his bitterness, desired the anonymity of being remembered only as an English poet to mock the way his critics viewed him. It's difficult to imagine such a self-regard for someone who wrote and left intact some of the most beautiful poetry ever written in English, but Keats obviously had his own shitbird to contend with, one that perhaps got in this last word. His acclaimed notion of negative capability, an idea that suggests that uncertainty and confusion can and will inspire, rather than oppose, creativity, isn't all that far removed from our notion that despair and self-contempt are opportunities for creative initiative. And nothing breeds uncertainty more than anger and the shame it so often creates. Nothing.

The black bird thrives in a state of permanent uncertainty, which it uses to anticipate and then smother creative excitement and appetite. Imagine then the force of will, the strength needed to inspire and sustain the refined lyrical resonance and creative intelligence that went into the creation of Keats's "Ode to a Nightingale," which so sensuously deals with that most tenuous, eternally resourceful state between sleep and waking, despite all the "bitterness of his heart."

> Forlorn! the very word is like a bell
>> To toll me back from thee to my sole self!
> Adieu! the fancy cannot cheat so well
>> As she is fam'd to do, deceiving elf.
> Adieu! adieu! thy plaintive anthem fades
>> Past the near meadows, over the still stream,
>>> Up the hill-side; and now 'tis buried deep
>>> In the next valley-glades:
>> Was it a vision, or a waking dream?
>> Fled is that music:—Do I wake or sleep?

I once became incensed while visiting the grave of a friend whose encouragement and criticism helped me write my book of poems *Failure*. Though I'd always loved the Baudelaire quote friends had put on his gravestone—*The dispersion and reconstitution of the self. / That's the whole story*—I now saw it as blatantly obscure and personally insulting. Yes, epitaph as slander. Why would he, so gifted, wise, and assiduous about all matters literary, want such an emblem to represent him for eternity? And how had I allowed it? I felt overcome with remorse and chagrin.

My friend had died abruptly of cancer shortly before my book was published and though I couldn't acknowledge it, I was left feeling abandoned and betrayed and, yes, angry. And having buried the anger along with the shame it created, I wasn't able to complete an elegy I'd spent years trying to write for him. Without realizing it, I'd come there that morning begging for inspiration and, perhaps, permission to finish my poem for him. And now, having erupted in anger for no real reason I could understand, I was overcome with shame and bewilderment, and began weeping. What sort of wretched person was I to be angry at a dear friend for dying two weeks before his fifty-second birthday? And just as suddenly as it'd erupted, the anger was gone, and these lines came:

> I've forgiven you, finally,
> for not living to see the book you helped me write
> get published. Only now do I understand that
> it's not the resentment I regret, it's the shame.

Lines that opened up into my elegy, "Welcome to the Springs," for my friend Robert Long. Anger, and the shame it caused, had blocked not only the grief but the forgiveness I was seeking. And then, not long after I finished this poem, I began wondering if there wasn't another way of helping my students overcome their own fears and misgivings. To confront in this same way emotions so difficult to even recognize. Yes, the same ominous emotions and the gravitational forces they created around them to repel further inspection seemed to discourage so many from even recognizing potentially powerful subject matter; once again, the shirtbird's most perverse and persuasive weapon, its invisibility. If you can't recognize your desire to deal with material that so often proves to be inspiring, you most certainly can't find the will to do so.

After struggling for years to find an exercise that might help students both realize and then deal with these constraints, I was surprised at the effect my teaching the Kafka book in our craft class had on so many of my students. Their excitement in seeing Kafka's persona get the better of his father inspired them to be more ambitious with their subject choices, and then my oldest son, Eli, introduced me to a book a friend of his had recommended for its fierce intimacy and political fervor, Édouard Louis's superbly political and moving tribute to his father, *Who Killed My Father*, which immediately struck me as being so different from and yet strangely similar to the Kafka book. Each book confronts its writer's most complex and passionate material by using familiar techniques in surprisingly original ways. Kafka uses the simple idea of a letter in an astonishingly prosecutorial and personal manner, while Louis uses in his memoir a similar kind of direct address to create a portrait of his father as a victim of the French class system in a style so tender and intimate it feels as if it's being acted out on a stage right before our eyes. Its first-person narrator imagines "a text for the theater" where "a father and son stand a few feet apart in a vast empty space" that could be a wheat field or a school gym, where "maybe it's snowing" and the snow buries them "until they disappear. The father and son almost never look at each other. The son is the only one to speak." They stand close and sometimes they touch but they somehow remain apart, and when the son, and only the son, speaks, "this does violence to them both." The father isn't allowed to tell his own story "while the son longs for a response that he will never receive." Yes, the same device of a speechless defendant being interrogated by the writer/prosecutor. The rest of the book follows these few precepts until the pain and sorrow of the boy's longing to know his father reveals an intimacy that was never allowed to evolve naturally, spontaneously; in Kafka's case due to the father's terror of losing the power of his emotional detachment, and in Louis's, the personal destruction wreaked by the French class system. Again, the exercise produced remarkable results, unlike from any one single exercise I'd previously given, other than the Kafka one. And since Louis acknowledges, among other books and films, the inspiration he derived from Peter Handke's very beautiful memoir of his mother's suicide, *A Sorrow beyond Dreams,* I decided to teach the Handke book next, which turned out to be an equally compelling source of inspiration.

The narrator, as in the two other books, is the writer himself, Handke, who serves as both the historian of his mother's recent suicide and the dramatist of his own difficulty in writing about it. Using novelistic narrative techniques, Handke directly addresses his reader in a blunt, lyrical, epistolary style that constantly shifts positions between his mother's story—peasants, he repeatedly tells us, she came from the German peasant class—and his own lower-to-middle-class childhood, and the writer/historian's sense of grief and bewilderment. It was exactly the kind of brilliant juggling act between artful transcendence and sheltering distance that proved so successful in the other books and now all I needed was the kind of idea that would connect the success of all three books in one exercise.

And since all three books to some degree take the shape of a kind of journal or diary, say the kind a John Cheever or Virginia Woolf wrote, it seemed prudent to ask my students to bring in a few pages of journal entries that addressed what they saw as their most pressing stories, using a persona narrator as their authors. The idea being that in using the journal form, which is designed to be read by only oneself, a private, unselfconscious form that creates the illusion of privacy, one can set aside one's ambitions and self-consciousness about publishing and be free of the fear of critical judgment and its repercussions. And by employing the kind of astute, fearless narrator all three writers used to bare their souls to the reader, my students also would be able to write successfully about the very kinds of subjects they weren't able to previously.

These journal exercises turned out to be the single most successful exercises I've ever used; in fact, my students refused to stop using them. Once they discovered and tamed what they so feared, the transfer over to poems and fiction was not only possible but much easier. The anger and shame that had so convincingly inhibited their desires were now allowed to speak through these personas, and to tell their remarkable stories.

OCCASIONALLY, WHEN SUGGESTING TO SOMEONE what might be hidden behind a strand of dialogue, an abbreviated scene and stanza, stuttering, coughing, or squirming erupts. Whatever is causing such upset, I may then suggest, might be seen as an opportunity to find an "I" or "We" or "You" brave, tolerant, and opinionated enough to confront the origins of their discontent. That inside their assembly of orchestrated personalities, the great democracy of voices we carry around within us, an "I" exists abundant enough to inhabit what Walt Whitman believed to be his own strength of vision: "I will effuse egotism and show it underlying all, and I will be the bard of personality. . . . And that all things of the universe are perfect miracles, each as profound as any." Yes, indeed, "the bard of personality" great enough to overcome all our foolishness and vain posturing, all the evidence of our greed and stupidity, so we might believe our one small voice is "as profound as any."

Left unexpressed, anger and its attendant passion, shame, engender only futility and failure. Without first realizing and then submitting to our fears and inadequacies, our ever-subservient and fragile vulnerability, there can be no catharsis, and thus, no poetry.

THE ARGUMENT AND THE LULLABY

At a party in New York in 1997, the poet Philip Levine asked me why Ralph Dickey and I never visited him in Fresno in 1972 as I'd told him we would. I did my best to explain it and he was kind enough to say he understood and was glad to finally know the reason after so many years. I wasn't sure why he asked, we'd known each other for years already, but I knew why I hadn't gone out of my way to explain it to him. It was too painful.

I was surprised when Ralph called me in Kalamazoo from Oakland over my spring break in 1972, surprised and alarmed. He'd sounded bad before but not like this. We'd managed to keep in touch since the late Sixties in San Francisco, but I hadn't seen him in two years now and he'd never sounded worse. He wouldn't say why exactly he was calling, only that he wanted to hear my voice, and I feared the worst and flew out there to see him. He was living, if you could call it that, in a small two-room place just outside of town, and his books, his piano, his job, and the woman he'd been living with were gone; under his shades he looked gutted, bruised, Talmudic, as if all his preceding suffering was only practice. Only the sheer drenched cloth of him remained, and a poetry book, *They Feed They Lion*, by Philip Levine, his favorite poet, lay on the floor near his feet. Yes, his favorite poet was a Jew from Detroit, one whose appetite for rage was famous. Neither of us ever questioned this fascination, but

I must have understood on some private level that the wildness of his admiration was no doubt inspired by his own unleashed anger. And hoping that Levine might remind him of the lion in himself that needed to be fed, I suggested we visit Levine. "Why would Levine want to see us, we haven't done anything," he answered. But now I was desperate, and without his permission, I looked Levine's number up in information—everyone in poetry knew he lived in Fresno—and called it, without even looking at Ralph. Fuck him, I thought, I didn't need his permission to save him. And when Levine answered, I stuttered something about how my friend Ralph, a really good poet, was also from Detroit, like him, had gone to Wayne State and Iowa, like him, and was friends with his friend, the poet Michael Harper, in one breathless whoosh, adding that Ralph really needed to see him. He didn't laugh or ask why, didn't want to know who I was or why I was speaking for someone else, and just said, sighing, "Okay, good, fine, come visit then! On Wednesday."

Maybe it was simple curiosity or intuitive goodness on his part, but neither Ralph nor I understood or questioned it, and the next morning we packed Ralph's rackety old VW and headed south toward Fresno, not knowing exactly where it was or how to get there. It wasn't that we didn't believe in maps, in our hurry and uncertainty it just never occurred to either of us to do anything as mundane and practical as worry about direction. Ralph also didn't seem to care if we got there or not, just the idea of going to see Levine was hopeful enough. After driving for some hours in the direction we assumed was right—south of the Bay Area—we stopped at a campground in Big Sur, which Phil later explained wasn't anywhere near Fresno, and, thinking we should probably eat something, I bought processed meat and a few potatoes at their market, all without speaking. Ralph had grown ever more silent and resentful that I'd talked him into this trip to "nowhere." That's how he now referred to this opportunity to see his favorite living poet, a "trip to nowhere." My silence had everything to do with my growing anger—how did I ever talk myself into spending my week off from teaching here, with him? We were a match all right: the Orpheus and Eurydice of poets, a marriage made in hell. It was suddenly clear to both of us, I thought, that silence was better than what was causing it. Which is when Ralph came up with the idea of smoking some hash he just happened to have with him. I hated drugs and almost never went near them, but for some reason I still don't understand, it suddenly seemed like a good idea. And then, a little later, while watching me cut potatoes for an inordinate amount of time over a fire neither of us seemed to particularly hold in high regard, he felt it necessary to explain in excruciating detail how Marie's face surfaced every time he made love to a woman, it didn't matter whom. He said it curiously, somewhat bemused, watching me for a reaction.

"I always thought you knew, and didn't care," he added.

Dropping the knife, I walked far into the silence of the redwoods, and started screaming. At the moment, the idea of my holding a knife was what frightened me most. He'd stared at it the whole time he told me all this.

The night grew suddenly darker, the sky higher, and the surrounding timberland more resoundingly silent. I stood there, in that embryonic darkness, shivering. It was all so clear suddenly: it was time to give up, just give up. He didn't want to be saved, by me, Levine, or fate. Encouragement was the last thing he wanted; coming this far was a last desperate act, for my benefit. He believed what I, too, often believed, that poetry only continued the pain, called further attention to our inability to rise above it. Saying the one thing his genius knew I couldn't resist, his shitbird had worn me down, had in fact won, if one could call complete surrender a victory. Cioran, whom Ralph had introduced me to, speaking of that "expatriate deluxe" Rilke, imagined the number of solitudes he had to accumulate in order "to be nowhere . . . extricate oneself from the world." Now we were both nowhere, lost in the midst of a vast primeval forest.

We returned to Oakland in silence. I didn't call Levine to explain or apologize. I wanted to but couldn't. What would I say— that death had won? That there was nothing left to save?

THIS MORNING, WALKING ALONG THE ocean on a splendid July morning here in East Hampton, I found myself eavesdropping on an argument between two strenuous points of view. I at first ignored the intrusion but then, looking around and seeing no one, realized that the argument was one I was having with myself, that once again I was trying to convince my friend Ralph Dickey that none of his reasons for such profound self-loathing were true or essential; once again I was attempting to find the perfect words that would finally convince him to hang on until the purpose of his existence could become as clear to him as it was to those of us who valued and loved him.

Everything else around me was calm and unassuming, barely a cloud in the sky. Everyone in my family was well and there was no other disturbance I could claim as a reason for this internal war of unyielding authorities. In any case, I knew all his arguments by heart: the ongoing plague of systemic racism, his many rejections and depressions, his unwillingness and incapacity to seek the kind of recognition and distinction so many of us wished for him, and of course, his endless infatuation with death: an obsession more urgent, sincere, and passionate than his poetry and music could compete with or endure. If art is a means of self-introduction, a trusted resource in the hazardous mission of self-knowledge, then death was his most faithful collaborator in that ambiguous and fecund state in which he lived most of his life; the state Keats so elegantly described in "Ode to a Nightingale": between waking and sleep. Even here, now, amid the exquisite beauty of the ocean, he remained obstinately indifferent to his gifts, sighing as I listed all his qualities and prizes—what did they matter, finally, he argued, showing me that superior smirk he seemed to reserve for me alone. His destiny, to die young, like Keats's name, was writ on water, and everyone except me seemed to know it.

Hadn't he said all this, everything, in a letter he wrote me after I left Iowa and he stayed to finish his degree, about a moment in our friendship when everything made sense, when we truly became essential friends? Yes, I remembered the letter well and the moment it was about. We drove down to the big reservoir outside Iowa City with two fellow students in the poetry program, two young women we liked, the four of us drinking vodka and walking around the edge of the reservoir, singing poems we all loved, by Neruda, Nazim Hikmet, Baudelaire, Rimbaud, and of course, Lorca—wonderful all-knowing, ever-evolving Federico García Lorca!

DELIRIUM

The day blurs
in the silent fields

Bee-eaters
sigh as they fly

The blue and white
distance
is delirious

The land has its arms
thrown wide

Ay lord lord
All this is too much

Singing into the icy December wind at the tops of our voices, all and each so young and full of love for the very idea of being poets . . . and then Ralph broke away and ran down some stairs to the semi-frozen lake below and began hopping over the ice like a true madman, waving his long arms about and hopping foot to foot, as if daring the fates to deny him such bliss. Then we all were running, hopping over the frozen water, singing and laughing ourselves hoarse, until we fell into one another's arms, drunk with what seemed an unending moment of joy we'd possess for the rest of our lives.

In any case, this is how I remembered this moment. In his letter, he remembered it somewhat differently:

Well, I'm still writing letters too carefully, like literary documents. What I want to say is that I'm unhappy. No, that doesn't mean anything. I'm dissatisfied. Except that it is not satisfaction that I want; it's joy. I am joyous when I'm reading work I already know and love, when I discover a new writer or a new work by an old writer, when I'm creating life with words. Most of the words form abortions, some of them are hideous. Stillbirths. One of which was forty pages. I tried to write the Reservoir story. What is the Reservoir story? It is on one hand the story of a moment in our friendship, and I wasn't willing or ready to examine the feelings of hatred and jealousy I had for you at that time. What I hated first of all was that you were actually trying to become my friend. That you wanted to know me. Impossible. How could you stoop so low as to value me that much? I was disgusted with you. I think I must still act with reservation with you. You, my best friend. The person I feel closest to. When I resist your criticism—about my poems, ideas, about the things we both value—it is because I still hate you for valuing me so much. This is not psychologizing. I know what I'm talking about.

"Yes, yes," I hear myself shouting back, "but how about the citywide piano-playing award you won as a high school senior in Detroit—a seventeen-year-old good enough to be chosen from thousands to play in Tiger Stadium, a major league baseball stadium!"

"There were hundreds there, not thousands, and I didn't win first prize . . . a white boy did . . ."

"But you won a full scholarship to Wayne State University and then a fellowship in science to study at Stanford and another to the Iowa Writers' Workshop—dammit! they put you up there on the stage before all of us first- and second-year students, showing you off as someone who'd just published his translation of Paul Celan's great Holocaust poem 'Death Fugue' in *Daedalus*, the most prestigious literary journal around . . ."

"But I never could publish any of my other translations of his poems . . ."

"You, the only student on the stage with all those famous writers, the pride and admiration on their faces that someone so young should be so gifted, possess such a bright future . . . We were all of us so proud and envious . . . How could someone so brilliant see himself as without worth—be so wrong?"

"Yes, okay, man," I can hear his shitbird answering, "but that guy up there with the elegant demeanor being held up as a standard didn't really exist, was a phantom, an illusion, it was all a role I played having to be someone, something to others, I always knew who, what I was—a boy not white or black or anything enough in between to be loved by his own mother . . .

"You want to know who I am, I once told you but you've forgotten—human beings love pain so let me share my pain with you—a private moment, a crisis, a moment of violence between me and . . . my first foster father hitting my foster mother . . . out of jealousy, to consolidate his position, to strike at the man his wife spoke with familiarly, out of fear she didn't love him anymore . . . because I betrayed her, because I wanted it to happen and said what was necessary for it to happen . . . to punish her for not being my real mother but a substitute . . .

" 'The world is ugly and the people are sad.' I think I must have said those lines to myself every day at least once a day since I first read them. Wallace Stevens said it. 'The world is ugly and the people are sad.' "

Yes, okay, fine, but the world also provides poetic geniuses like Stevens and, in my humble opinion, you, Ralph. It is indeed ugly and sad and incommensurably beautiful, almost too much to behold. This one image of you playing your version of "Round Midnight" at a bar in Iowa one night—how you just stood up from the bar and went over to the piano in the corner and started playing like it'd all been arranged ahead of time, one moment we were talking about poetry and women and the next you were at that piano, your eyes closed, a cigarette dangling off your bottom lip, busy making a sound so ethereal and piercing, so intimate and full of prophecy and yearning it no longer had anything to do with Monk or Coltrane or Rilke or anyone else, just you, Ralph, just you making music so pure everyone stopped talking and drinking and breathing and just sat there staring . . . at you, the almond-skinned young man perched on the edge of a piano bench, not knowing I or anyone else existed, sitting there doing the one thing you liked most to do, make music so fine God was probably looking down at you like some idea of bliss come alive, thinking what all the rest of us were thinking: that what we were hearing wasn't coming out of that old rickety upright bar piano, or even out of the pianist himself, it was arising out of the floor and walls, down through that water-stained ceiling, coming from a place beyond and deeper and more unforgiving than anything any of us had ever heard before, a place so fragile, so elegant, there was nothing and nowhere before or after, only this one moment that would soon end and return to wherever it came from, as if it knew what we all knew: that it was just too beautiful and fragile to survive . . .

. . . like the stillborn lullaby he wrote as a last goodbye:

MULATTO LULLABY

Be my stillborn son my son
So the doctors will haul you
Out to the world
And whip your skin to suede

Be my stillborn son my son
So the flies will land
On your wet glass eyes
And wade like cranes

Be my stillborn son my son
So the flies will deposit
Their pouches of maggots
Mouthfuls of rice

Son born stillborn
Float in the jar
Like you soaked in my womb

WHAT WE WANT

Once, new to the city, someone at a literary event said something I've never forgotten, said it loudly enough for everyone around him to hear: "Everyone here wants something." I didn't have any idea what he was referring to exactly, but I looked around the crowded room, to see what he was seeing. I'd been advised by more than one person that, being a young writer in Manhattan, it was expedient, at the very least, to make use of every opportunity to advance myself—was this the sort of thing he was referring to? Many in the room were accomplished writers, while others appeared to be auditioning for the part; all, however, displayed the kind of professional élan that made them look as if they belonged here, or at least believed so. In any case, everywhere I looked I saw evidence of my invisibility: Susan Sontag standing nearby, talking heatedly to Joseph Brodsky, who didn't appear to be equally committed to whatever so engrossed her, while Grace Paley, off to his left, was arguing with someone who looked like Gore Vidal, while several reputations away, back near the front windows, Derek Walcott was bent over in laughter, as he so often was, while talking to Toni Morrison, who seemed perfectly delighted by his merriment. To feel less self-conscious and obvious, I moved across the room to what I hoped was a less critical and terrifying view of the proceedings. But it was too late. I couldn't stop wondering what it was I wanted: some sort of obvious, great, or middling success, or some smaller notion about self-satisfaction? Maybe it was the kind of satisfaction and joy Ralph referred to in his letter: the joy he felt when he was "reading work I already know and love, when I discover a new writer or a new work by an old writer, when I'm creating life with words . . ."

Isn't this what everyone here wanted, too—to feel the joy of knowing that they were doing something only they could do, something that somehow magically defined and presented them to the world, something maybe they were ordained to do?

Is that what inspired us to take on and perform so presumptuous and impractical an ideal—bound us all so tightly together on so tiny a sanctuary island, that so compelled us we never wanted to do anything or be anyone else?

And it was then, in the midst of this self-inquisition, that I, along with everyone else around me, heard a loud banging noise coming from somewhere in the middle of the room and, as if choreographed, all simultaneously stepped back, opening a circle in the center of which knelt a young woman, pounding the heel of her shoe against the floor, her black curly hair bouncing wildly from side to side, as if keeping time with the blows. Did I know her, I wondered, her magnificent hair looked familiar. In unison we all stepped forward for a closer look at this young comedian seal, performing an act so wonderfully contrived it seemed both innocent and infinitely vain—what was it she wanted: glory, admiration, to be counted among the elite, if only for a moment?

When I tell someone this story, they often look horrified. How could anyone behave in so crass a manner? their eyes seem to ask. Yes, crass perhaps, but the passion is memorable, genuine and prepossessing. Here at my desk, I can still hear the echoing blasts of her shoe against hardwood, see her mane of fierce black hair, the sparkle in her black eyes as she stopped her hammering and shyly looked up and around at us, her jury of fellow messenger angels, all staring down at her, as she slowly, with exquisite ease, rose to her feet, curtsied, and then quickly vanished into the past.

Occasionally, sitting alone at night in front of a TV, I'll turn the sound off, and try to imagine the plight of the characters, who, freed of dialogue and unburdened by plot, speak with their eyes and hands, lip-synching my thoughts as they wander in and out of their delirious high jinks and brutal interactions, these countless nomadic tribes of killers, lovers, imposters, war heroes, and clueless fall guys, performing their sad, hopeless pantomimes, each a comedian seal, a persona too vulnerable, ignorant, or unforgiving to survive, each a dilemma no one can solve or redeem, an argument and a lullaby impossible to remember or forget.

Is this why it feels like a small death every time I fail myself or someone else, why I can't give up on an idea or feeling even when it's wise to do so, when I know I've taken myself as far as I can or should go, that I'm hopping over thin ice . . .

. . . why it's so important to me that I or all my friends and students not surrender to this dark voice, why I can't forgive the anger I felt when Ralph abandoned us . . . the anger and shame . . .

. . . why I turned his music, his yearning, and his life into an argument I can't win or lose, into the lullaby he was playing that night, so slowly, sweetly, painfully . . .

. . . yes, isn't this what we all want, finally, not fame, recognition, or adoration, but confirmation, evidence, some small sample of proof that we—even if for only a moment—not only exist but matter? Isn't this what all the hammering is about, finally—the splendid sound Ralph made that one night, the forgiving amends and affirmations, or, simply, the comforts of the abyss?

Acknowledgments

I began writing this book back in 2003, though I could easily claim that the idea behind it began much earlier, with my childhood obsession with masks. I can't remember a time when I wasn't fascinated with masks, the ones we hide behind and those we create as friends, sources of inspiration, and companions. I can remember discussing Oscar Wilde's famous observation about them—"Man is least himself when he talks in his own person. Give him a mask, and he will tell you the truth"—with Herbert Wilner, the novelist and director of the creative writing program at San Francisco State College, where I was an undergraduate student, in 1966. How enthusiastically he listened to my enraptured testaments about how the first-person narrators we were studying were actually masks for the writers creating them. Yes, masks and persona narrators, dual obsessions that eventually took their shape as a writing method and a school of creative writing. Over these many years many generous friends, colleagues, and students have patiently listened to me discuss the various ideas and theories that have slowly and resolutely evolved into The Writers Studio. The late James

Tuttleton, the chairman of the English department at NYU, who, after laughing at my nervous jokes about the masks poets such as Walt Whitman and Emily Dickinson wore, hired me to teach one undergraduate poetry-writing class at NYU in 1978. The poet he was hiring to teach didn't yet possess a published book or much of a résumé. And the prescience of John Maynard, also of NYU, whose faith and wisdom guided the creation of a remarkable and lasting graduate department of creative writing. Howard Moss, poetry editor at *The New Yorker*, who took me to lunch at the Algonquin Hotel and introduced me to the literary world of New York City. Richard Howard, who kindly published an early poem of mine about movie extras, "Strangers in Old Photographs," in *American Review* (volume 22) in 1975. Yes, movie extras, those anonymous beings that serve as stand-ins and ornaments to our various pretensions and realities, an early incarnation of my obsession with persona narrators. His brilliant translation of E. M. Cioran's *The Temptation to Exist*, the book that inspired the later drafts of my present book, also provided its title.

Gratitude also to the many good souls who have shown me generosity during the writing of this book. The encouragement and inspiration I received from friends and colleagues who happily indulged my obsession during wonderful lunches and dinners: Lawrence Joseph, Grace Schulman, Kathryn Court, Cornelius Eady, Alice Quinn, Yusef Komunyakaa, and Major Jackson. I am most grateful to my fellow teachers and friends at The Writers Studio who either read versions of this book or helped organize and inspire its ideas: Liz Kingsley, Cynthia Weiner, Lesley Dormen, Joel Hinman, Isabelle Deconinck, Lisa Bellamy, Martha Qualben, Michele Herman, Rachel Nevins, Scott Hunter, Peter Krass, and Lucinda Holt. I am also indebted to Mark Peterson, Eleanor Kedney, Nancy

Matsunaga, Gail Ford, Reneé Bibby, Therese Eiben, Anamyn Turowski, Sylvie Bertrand, Doris Chang, Elliot Satsky, Nicola Bultrini, and Stas' Gawronski, who extended this idea from New York City to Tucson, San Francisco, Amsterdam, Hudson Valley, New Jersey, Rome, and online; our first teachers who paved the way: Elliot Figman, Harold Marcus, Lisa Kaufman, Amy Dana, Elizabeth England, Frazier Russell, Joanne Naiman, Andree Lockwood, Sarah McElwain, Sheila Welch, and Abby Wender; and Rebecca Gee, who ran our Kids Write nonprofit branch.

And for the inspiration and encouragement of our advisory board: Yehuda Amichai (in memoriam), Jill Bialosky, Kathryn Court, Carl Dennis, Cornelius Eady, Jennifer Egan, Marc Frons, Julia Glass, Bill Henderson, Edward Hirsch, Matthew Klam, Robert Pinsky, Kimberly Reed, Grace Schulman, and Rosanna Warren.

I wish also to thank Willard Cook, founder of *Epiphany*, who published *The Writers Studio at 30*, and its editors, Odette Heideman, Peter Krass, and Lisa Bellamy; and Rich McKnight, longtime website designer and friend, who created our first website and online classroom and continues to be a valued adviser.

And particular gratitude to the remarkable patience of friends who read through any number of drafts and made so many helpful suggestions: Marc Frons, James Lasdun, Drenka Willen, Edward Hirsch, Ronald Sharp, and Robert Pinsky; and my agent, Georges Borchardt, who provided much-needed guidance and illumination. And a true guardian angel, Jill Bialosky, my editor at W. W. Norton, who helped me realize the final form of this book, encouraging me to enlarge and enrich the original idea into a more meaningful life story. And her assistant, Drew Elizabeth Weitman, who in so many ways was instrumental in helping this manuscript become a finished book.

My most profound gratitude goes to my wife, Monica Banks, who provided me with that most essential of realms, a home, and recognized what I was struggling to write long before I did. And our sons, Eli and Augie, whose sympathy and understanding is a constant reminder of what a truly lucky man I am. And the early comforting mentorship and attendance of Michael S. Harper, who more than once reminded me of the importance of wearing a hat in winter—"90 percent of the body's heat is lost through the head," he would sing, trying to appear stern and not laugh. And finally, Michael's other disciple, my dear late friend Ralph Dickey, whose brief life inspired the very idea of this book and school, and whose spirit provides lasting comfort.

THE CHAPTER "ANGER AND SHAME" will appear in *Driven to Write: Psychological Perspectives*, a collection of personal essays about writing edited by Drs. Ellen Pinsky and Michael Slevin.

Credits